Workshop on Monolingual Text-To-Text Generation 2011

Held at ACL HLT 2011

Portland, Oregon, USA
24 June 2011

ISBN: 978-1-61839-252-7

Printed from e-media with permission by:

Curran Associates, Inc.
57 Morehouse Lane
Red Hook, NY 12571

CURRAN ASSOCIATES INC. proceedings.com

Some format issues inherent in the e-media version may also appear in this print version.

Printed by Curran Associates, Inc. (2011)

For permission requests, please contact the Association for Computational Linguistics at the address below.

Association for Computational Linguistics
209 N. Eighth Street
Stroudsburg, Pennsylvania 18360

Phone: 1-570-476-8006
Fax: 1-570-476-0860

acl@aclweb.org

Additional copies of this publication are available from:

Curran Associates, Inc.
57 Morehouse Lane
Red Hook, NY 12571 USA
Phone: 845-758-0400
Fax: 845-758-2634
Email: curran@proceedings.com
Web: www.proceedings.com

Introduction

The ability to perform monolingual text-to-text generation is an important step in solving many natural language processing problems. For example, when generating novel text at the sentence-level, abstractive summarization systems may need to compress sentences or fuse multiple sentences together; the evaluation of translation systems may require additional paraphrases to use as reference gold standards; and answers to questions may need to be generated automatically from extracted sentences.

The community of researchers examining monolingual text-to-text generation has grown steadily in recent years, introducing the need for a focused venue to communicate results in this area. To this end, we proposed and organised this workshop at ACL with endorsement from SIGGEN. We hope that this is the first of many text-to-text generation workshops to come.

We were excited to receive 18 submissions which were judged in accordance with the standard reviewing practices of the ACL 2011 main conference. As we intended that the workshop serve as a new forum for the community, our aim in the selection process was to choose high quality papers which would spark discussion amongst the participants.

We selected seven long papers and four short papers. Together, they tackle a diverse range of research questions: reflecting upon the scope of what might be generated in a text-to-text process, examining new generation methods, and addressing the ever challenging issue of evaluation.

We would like to thank everyone involved in the preparation of this workshop. We were very happy to receive such an enthusiastic response from the community when we proposed the workshop. We would specifically like to thank Noah Smith for his invited talk. We would also like to thank the reviewers who helped us to put together this wonderful program. Finally, we are grateful for the guidance provided by the steering committee on the direction of this workshop.

We hope you find the program challenging and the resulting discussion engaging.

Katja and Stephen

Organizers:

Katja Filippova, Google
Stephen Wan, CSIRO

Program Committee:

Anja Belz, University of Brighton
Bernd Bohnet, University of Stuttgart
Aoife Cahill, University of Stuttgart
Chris Callison-Burch, Johns Hopkins University
Robert Dale, Macquarie University
Mark Dras, Macquarie University
Michel Galley, Microsoft
Kevin Knight, University of Southern California, ISI
Emiel Krahmer, Tilburg University
Mirella Lapata, University of Edinburgh
Nitin Madnani, ETS
Erwin Marsi, NTNU
Kathleen McKeown, Columbia University
Ryan McDonald, Google
Cécile Paris, CSIRO
Michael Strube, HITS
Michael White, Ohio State University
David Zajic, University of Maryland

Invited Speaker:

Noah Smith, Carnegie Mellon University

Table of Contents

Conference Program

Friday June 24, 2011

Session 1: 9:00 - 10:30

Learning to Simplify Sentences Using Wikipedia
Will Coster and David Kauchak

Web-based Validation for Contextual Targeted Paraphrasing
Houda Bouamor, Aurélien Max, Gabriel Illouz and Anne Vilnat

An Unsupervised Alignment Algorithm for Text Simplification Corpus Construction
Stefan Bott and Horacio Saggion

Comparing Phrase-based and Syntax-based Paraphrase Generation
Sander Wubben, Erwin Marsi, Antal van den Bosch and Emiel Krahmer

Morning break: 10:30 - 11:00

Invited Talk (Noah Smith) and Discussion: 11:00 - 12:30

Lunch break: 12:30 - 14:00

Session 3: 14:00 - 15:30

Text Specificity and Impact on Quality of News Summaries
Annie Louis and Ani Nenkova

Towards Strict Sentence Intersection: Decoding and Evaluation Strategies
Kapil Thadani and Kathleen McKeown

Learning to Fuse Disparate Sentences
Micha Elsner and Deepak Santhanam

Friday June 24, 2011 (continued)

Afternoon break: 15:30 - 16:00

Session 4: 16:00 - 17:30

Framework for Abstractive Summarization using Text-to-Text Generation
Pierre-Etienne Genest and Guy Lapalme

Creating Disjunctive Logical Forms from Aligned Sentences for Grammar-Based Paraphrase Generation
Scott Martin and Michael White

Paraphrastic Sentence Compression with a Character-based Metric: Tightening without Deletion
Courtney Napoles, Chris Callison-Burch, Juri Ganitkevitch and Benjamin Van Durme

Evaluating Sentence Compression: Pitfalls and Suggested Remedies
Courtney Napoles, Benjamin Van Durme and Chris Callison-Burch

Learning to Simplify Sentences Using Wikipedia

William Coster
Computer Science Department
Pomona College
wpc02009@pomona.edu

David Kauchak
Computer Science Department
Pomona College
dkauchak@cs.pomona.edu

Abstract

In this paper we examine the sentence simplification problem as an English-to-English translation problem, utilizing a corpus of 137K aligned sentence pairs extracted by aligning English Wikipedia and Simple English Wikipedia. This data set contains the full range of transformation operations including rewording, reordering, insertion and deletion. We introduce a new translation model for text simplification that extends a phrase-based machine translation approach to include phrasal deletion. Evaluated based on three metrics that compare against a human reference (BLEU, word-F1 and SSA) our new approach performs significantly better than two text compression techniques (including T3) and the phrase-based translation system without deletion.

1 Introduction

In this paper we examine the sentence simplification problem: given an English sentence we aim to produce a simplified version of that sentence with simpler vocabulary and sentence structure while preserving the main ideas in the original sentence (Feng, 2008). The definition what a "simple" sentence is can vary and represents a spectrum of complexity and readability. For concreteness, we use Simple English Wikipedia[1] as our archetype of simplified English. Simple English Wikipedia articles represent a simplified version of traditional English Wikipedia articles. The main Simple English Wikipedia page outlines general guidelines for creating simple articles:

- *Use Basic English vocabulary and shorter sentences. This allows people to understand normally complex terms or phrases.*
- *Simple does not mean short. Writing in Simple English means that simple words are used. It does not mean readers want basic information. Articles do not have to be short to be simple; expand articles, add details, but use basic vocabulary.*

The data set we examine contains aligned sentence pairs of English Wikipedia[2] with Simple English Wikipedia (Coster and Kauchak, 2011; Zhu et al., 2010). We view the simplification problem as an English-to-English translation problem: given aligned sentence pairs consisting of a normal, unsimplified sentence and a simplified version of that sentence, the goal is to learn a sentence simplification system to "translate" from normal English to simplified English. This setup has been successfully employed in a number of text-to-text applications including machine translation (Och and Ney, 2003), paraphrasing (Wubben et al., 2010) and text compression (Knight and Marcu, 2002; Cohn and Lapata, 2009).

Table 1 shows example sentence pairs from the aligned data set. One of the challenges of text simplification is that, unlike text compression where the emphasis is often on word deletion, text simplifica-

[1] http://simple.wikipedia.org

[2] http://en.wikipedia.org/

a.	Normal: Simple:	Greene agreed that she could earn more by *breaking away from* 20th Century Fox. Greene agreed that she could earn more by *leaving* 20th Century Fox.
b.	Normal: Simple:	The crust and *underlying relatively rigid* mantle make up the lithosphere. The crust and mantle make up the lithosphere.
c.	Normal: Simple:	They *established themselves here and* called that port Menestheus's port. They called the port Menestheus's port.
d.	Normal: Simple:	Heat engines are often confused with the cycles they attempt to mimic. *Real* heat engines are often confused with the *ideal engines or* cycles they attempt to mimic.
e.	Normal: Simple:	*In 1962* , Steinbeck *received* the Nobel Prize *for* Literature. Steinbeck *won* the Nobel Prize *in* Literature *in 1962*.

Table 1: Example aligned sentences from English Wikipedia and Simple English Wikipedia. *Normal* refers an English Wikipedia sentence and *Simple* to a corresponding Simple English Wikipedia sentence.

tion involves the full range of transformation operations:

deletion: "*underlying relatively rigid*" in **b.**, "*established themselves here and*" in **c.** and the comma in **d.**

rewording: "*breaking away from*" → "*leaving*" in **a.** and "*received*" → "*won*" in **e.**

reordering: in **e.** "*in 1962*" moves from the beginning of the sentence to the end.

insertion: "*ideal engines or*" in **d.**

Motivated by the need to model all of these different transformations, we chose to extend a statistical phrase-based translation system (Koehn et al., 2007). In particular, we added phrasal deletion to the probabilistic translation model. This addition broadens the deletion capabilities of the system since the base model only allows for deletion *within* a phrase. As Kauchak and Coster (2011) point out, deletion is a frequently occurring phenomena in the simplification data.

There are a number of benefits of text simplification research. Much of the current text data available including Wikipedia, news articles and most web pages are written with an average adult reader as the target audience. Text simplification can make this data available to a broader range of audiences including children, language learners, the elderly, the hearing impaired and people with aphasia or cognitive disabilities (Feng, 2008; Carroll et al., 1998). Text simplification has also been shown to improve the performance of other natural language processing applications including semantic role labeling (Vickrey and Koller, 2008) and relation extraction (Miwa et al., 2010).

2 Previous Work

Most previous work in the area of sentence simplification has not been from a data-driven perspective. Feng (2008) gives a good historical overview of prior text simplification systems including early rule-based approaches (Chandrasekar and Srinivas, 1997; Carroll et al., 1998; Canning et al., 2000) and a number of commercial approaches. Vickrey and Koller (2008) and Miwa et al. (2010) employ text simplification as a preprocessing step, though both use manually generated rules.

Our work extends recent work by Zhu et al. (2010) that also examines Wikipedia/Simple English Wikipedia as a data-driven, sentence simplification task. They propose a probabilistic, syntax-based approach to the problem and compare against a baseline of no simplification and a phrase-based translation approach. They show improvements with their approach on target-side only metrics including Flesch readability and n-gram language model perplexity, but fail to show improvements for their approach on evaluation metrics that compare against a human reference simplification. In contrast, our approach achieves statistically significant improvements for three different metrics that compare against human references.

Sentence simplification is closely related to the

problem of sentence compression, another English-to-English translation task. Knight and Marcu (2002) were one of the first to formalize text compression as a data-driven problem and proposed a probabilistic, noisy-channel model and decision tree-based model for compression. Galley and McKeown (2007) show improvements to the noisy-channel approach based on rule lexicalization and rule Markovization. Recently, a number of approaches to text compression have been proposed that score transformation rules discriminatively based on support vector machines (McDonald, 2006; Cohn and Lapata, 2009) and conditional random fields (Nomoto, 2007; Nomoto, 2008) instead of using maximum likelihood estimation. With the exception of Cohn and Lapata (2009), all of these text compression approaches make the simplifying assumption that the compression process happens only via word deletion. We provide comparisons with some of these systems, however, for text simplification where lexical changes and reordering are frequent, most of these techniques are not appropriate.

Our proposed approach builds upon approaches employed in machine translation (MT). We introduce a variant of a phrase-based machine translation system (Och and Ney, 2003; Koehn et al., 2007) for text simplification. Although MT systems that employ syntactic or hierarchical information have recently shown improvements over phrase-based approaches (Chiang, 2010), our initial investigation with syntactically driven approaches showed poorer performance on the text simplification task and were less robust to noise in the training data.

Both English Wikipedia and Simple English Wikipedia have received recent analysis as a possible corpus by for both sentence compression and simplification. Yamangil and Nelken (2008) examine the history logs of English Wikipedia to learn sentence compression rules. Yatskar et al. (2010) learn a set of candidate phrase simplification rules based on edit changes identified in both Wikipedias revision histories, though they only provide a list of the top phrasal rules and do not utilize them in an end-to-end simplification system. Napoles and Dredze (2010) provide an analysis of the differences between documents in English Wikipedia and Simple English Wikipedia, though they do not view the data set as a parallel corpus.

3 Text Simplification Corpus

Few data sets exist for text simplification and data sets for the related task of sentence compression are small, containing no more than a few thousand aligned sentence pairs (Knight and Marcu, 2002; Cohn and Lapata, 2009; Nomoto, 2009). For this paper, we utilized a sentence-aligned corpus generated by aligning English Wikipedia with Simple English Wikipedia resulting in 137K aligned sentence pairs. This data set is larger than any previously examined for sentence simplification and orders of magnitude larger than those previously examined for sentence compression.

We give a brief overview of the corpus generation process here. For more details and an analysis of the data set, see (Coster and Kauchak, 2011). Throughout this article we will refer to English Wikipedia articles/sentences as **normal** and Simple English Wikipedia articles as **simple**.

We aligned the normal and simple articles at the document level based on exact match of the title and then removed all article pairs that were stubs, disambiguation pages, meta-pages or only contained a single line. Following a similar approach to previous monolingual alignment techniques (Barzilay and Elhadad, 2003; Nelken and Shieber, 2006), we then aligned each simple paragraph to any normal paragraph that had a normalized TF-IDF cosine similarity above a set threshold. These aligned paragraphs were then aligned at the sentence level using a dynamic programming approach, picking the best sentence-level alignment from a combination of the following sentence-level alignments:

- normal sentence inserted
- normal sentence deleted
- one normal sentence to one simple sentence
- two normal sentences to one simple sentence
- one normal sentence to two simple sentence

Following Nelken and Shieber (2006), we used TF-IDF cosine similarity to measure the similarity between aligned sentences and only kept aligned sentence pairs with a similarity threshold above 0.5. We found this thresholding approach to be more intuitive than trying to adjust a skip (insertion or deletion) penalty, which has also been proposed (Barzilay and Elhadad, 2003).

4 Simplification Model

Given training data consisting of aligned normal-simple sentence pairs, we aim to produce a translation system that takes as input a normal English sentence and produces a simplified version of that sentence. Motivated by the large number and importance of lexical changes in the data set, we chose to use a statistical phrase-based translation system. We utilized a modified version of Moses, which was originally developed for machine translation (Koehn et al., 2007).

Moses employs a log-linear model, which can be viewed as an extension of the noisy channel model and combines a phrase-based translation model, an n-gram language model, as well as a number of other models/feature functions to identify the best translation/simplification. The key component of Moses is the phrase-based translation model which decomposes the probability calculation of a normal sentence simplifying to a simple sentence as the product of individual phrase translations:

$$p(\text{simple}|\text{normal}) = \prod_{i=1}^{m} p(\bar{s_i}|\bar{n_i})$$

where each $\bar{s_i}$ is a phrase (one or more contiguous words) in the simple sentence and $\bar{s_1}, \bar{s_2}, ..., \bar{s_m}$ exactly cover the simple sentence. $\bar{n_i}$ are similarly defined over the normal sentence. $p(\bar{s_i}|\bar{n_i})$ denotes the probability of a normal phrase being translated/simplified to the corresponding simplified phrase. These phrasal probabilities are extracted from the sentence pairs based on an EM-learned word alignment using GIZA++ (Och and Ney, 2000).

Phrase-based models in machine translation often require that both phrases in the phrasal probabilities contain one or more words, since phrasal deletion/insertion is rare and can complicate the decoding process. For text simplification, however, phrasal deletion commonly occurs: 47% of the sentence pairs contain deletions (Coster and Kauchak, 2011). To model this deletion, we relax the restriction that the simple phrase must be non-empty and include in the translation model probabilistic phrasal deletion rules of the form $p(NULL|\bar{n_i})$ allowing for phrases to be deleted during simplification.

To learn these phrasal deletions within Moses, we modify the original word alignment output from GIZA++ before learning the phrase table entries in two ways:

1. If one or more contiguous normal words are unaligned in the original alignment, we align them to NULL appropriately inserted on the simple side

2. If a set of normal words N all align to a single simple word s and there exists an $n \in N$ where $n = s$ then for all $n' \in N : n' \neq n$ we align them to NULL.

This second modification has two main benefits. Frequently, if a word occurs in both the normal and simple sentence and it is aligned to itself, no other words should be aligned to that word. As others have noted, this type of spurious alignment is particularly prevalent with function words, which tend to occur in many different contexts (Chen et al., 2009). Second, even in situations where it may be appropriate for multiple words to align to a single word (for example, in compound nouns, such as *President Obama* $\rightarrow$ *Obama*), removing the alignment of the extra words, allows us to delete those words in other contexts. We lose some specificity with this adaptation because some deletions can now occur independent of context, however, empirically this modification provides more benefit than hindrance for the model. We conjecture that the language model helps avoid these problematic cases.

Table 2 shows excerpts from an example sentence pair before the alignment alteration and after. In the original alignment "*, aka Rodi*" is unaligned. After the alignment processing, the unaligned phrase is mapped to NULL allowing for the possibility of learning a phrasal deletion entry in the phrase table. We also modified the decoder to appropriately handle NULL mappings during the translation process.

Table 3 shows a sample of the phrasal deletion rules learned. These rules and probabilities were learned by the original phrase-table generation code

Normal:	Sergio Rodriguez Garcia , *aka Rodri* , is a spanish footballer ...
Simple:	Sergio Rodriguez Garcia is a spanish football player ...
Modified Simple:	Sergio Rodriguez Garcia NULL is a spanish football player ...

Table 2: Example output from the alignment modification step to capture phrasal deletion. Words that are vertically aligned are aligned in the word alignment.

Phrase-table entry			prob
,	→	NULL	0.057
the	→	NULL	0.033
of the	→	NULL	0.0015
or	→	NULL	0.0014
however ,	→	NULL	0.00095
the city of	→	NULL	0.00034
generally	→	NULL	0.00033
approximately	→	NULL	0.00025
, however ,	→	NULL	0.00022
, etc	→	NULL	0.00013

Table 3: Example phrase-table entries learned from the data and their associated probability.

of Moses after the word alignment was modified. The highest probability rules tend to delete punctuation and function words, however, other phrases also appeared. 0.5% of the rules learned during training are deletion rules.

5 Experiments

We compared five different approaches on the text simplification task:

none: Does no simplification. Outputs the normal, unsimplified sentence.

K & M: Noisy-channel sentence compression system described in Knight and Marcu (2002).

T3: Synchronous tree substitution grammar, trained discriminatively (Cohn and Lapata, 2009).

Moses: Phrase-based, machine translation approach (Koehn et al., 2007).

Moses+Del: Our approach described in Section 4 which is a phrase-based approach with the addition of phrasal deletion.

From the aligned data set of 137K sentence pairs, we used 124K for training and 1,300 for testing with the remaining 12K sentences used during development. We trained the n-gram language model used by the last four systems on the simple side of the training data.[3] T3 requires parsed data which we generated using the Stanford parser (Klein and Manning, 2003). Both Moses and Moses+Del were trained using the default Moses parameters and we used the last 500 sentence pairs from the training set to optimize the hyper-parameters of the log-linear model for both Moses variants. T3 was run with the default parameters.

Due to runtime and memory issues, we were unable to run T3 on the full data set.[4] We therefore present results for T3 trained on the largest training set that completed successfully, the first 30K sentence pairs. This still represents a significantly larger training set than T3 has been run on previously. For comparison, we also provide results below for Moses+Del trained on the same 30K sentences.

5.1 Evaluation

Since there is no standard way of evaluating text simplification, we provide results for three different automatic methods, all of which compare the system's output to a reference simplification. We used BLEU (Papineni et al., 2002), which is the weighted mean of n-gram precisions with a penalty for brevity. It has been used extensively in machine translation and has been shown to correlate well with human performance judgements.

We also adopt two automatic measures that have been used to evaluate text compression that compare the system's output to a reference translation

[3]See (Turner and Charniak, 2005) for a discussion of problems that can occur for text compression when using a language model trained on data from the uncompressed side.

[4]On 30K sentences T3 took 4 days to train. On the full data set, we ran T3 for a week and at that point the discriminative training was using over 100GB of memory and we terminated the run.

System	BLEU	word-F1	SSA
none	0.5937	0.5967	0.6179
K & M	0.4352	0.4352	0.4871
T3*	0.2437	0.2190	0.3651
Moses	0.5987	0.6076	0.6224
Moses+Del	0.6046	0.6149	0.6259

Table 4: Performance of the five approaches on the test data. All differences in performance are statistically significant. * - T3 was only trained on 30K sentence pairs for performance reasons.

(Clarke and Lapata, 2006): simple string accuracy measure (a normalized version of edit distance, abbreviated SSA) and F1 score calculated over words. We calculated F1 over words instead of grammatical relations (subject, direct/indirect object, etc.) since finding the relation correspondence between the system output and the reference is a non-trivial task for simplification data where reordering, insertions and lexical changes can occur. Clarke and Lapata (2006) showed a moderate correlation with human judgement for SSA and a strong correlation for the F1 measure.

To measure whether the difference between system performance is statistically significant, we use bootstrap resampling with 100 samples with the t-test (Koehn, 2004).

5.2 Results

Table 4 shows the results on the test set for the different evaluation measures. All three of the evaluation metrics rank the five systems in the same order with Moses+Del performing best. All differences between the systems are statistically significant for all metrics at the $p = 0.01$ level. One of the challenges for the sentence simplification problem is that, like sentence compression, not making any changes to the system produces reasonable results (contrast this with machine translation). In the test set, 30% of the simple sentences were the same as the corresponding normal sentence. Because of this, we see that not making any changes (*none*) performs fairly well. It is, however, important to leave these sentences in the test set, since not all sentences need simplification and systems should be able to handle these sentences appropriately.

Both of the text compression systems perform poorly on the text simplification task with results that are significantly worse than doing nothing. Both of these systems tended to bias towards modifying the sentences (T3 modified 77% of the sentences and K & M 96%). For K & M, the poor results are not surprising since the model only allows for deletion operations and is more tailored to the compression task. Although T3 does allow for the full range of simplification operations, it was often overly aggressive about deletion, for example T3 simplified:

> *There was also a proposal for an extension from Victoria to Fulham Broadway station on the district line , but this was not included in the bill .*

to "*it included .*" Overall, the output of T3 averaged 13 words per sentence, which is significantly lower than the gold standard's 21 words per sentence. T3 also suffered to a lesser extent from inappropriately inserting words/phrases, which other researchers have also noted (Nomoto, 2009). Some of these issues were a results of T3's inability to cope with noise in the test data, both in the text or the parses.

Both Moses and Moses+Del perform better than the text compression systems as well as the baseline system, *none*. If we remove those sentences in the test set where the simple sentence is the same as the normal sentence and only examine those sentences where a simplification should occur, the difference between the phrase-based approaches and *none* is even more significant with BLEU scores of 0.4560, 0.4723 and 0.4752, for *none*, Moses and Moses+Del respectively.

If we compare Moses and Moses+Del, the addition of phrasal deletion results in a statistically significant improvement. The phrasal deletion was a common operation in the simplifications made by Moses+Del; in 8.5% of the test sentences, Moses+Del deleted at least one phrase. To better understand this performance difference, Table 5 shows the BLEU scores for sentences where each respective system made a change (i.e. the output simplification is different than the input). In both cases, when the systems make simplifications on sentences that should be simplified, we see large gains in the output over doing nothing. While Moses improves over the baseline of doing nothing by 0.047 BLEU,

		BLEU	
System	Case	*none*	output
Moses	correct change	0.4431	0.4901
	incorrect change	1	0.8625
Moses+Del	correct change	0.4087	0.4788
	incorrect change	1	0.8706

Table 5: BLEU scores for Moses and Moses+Del on sentences where the system made a change. "correct change" shows the score where a change was made by the system as well as in the reference and "incorrect change" where a change was made by the system, but not the reference.

	BLEU	
System	original	oracle
Moses	0.5987	0.6317
Moses+Del	0.6046	0.6421

Table 7: BLEU score for the original system versus the best possible "oracle" translations generated by greedily selecting the best translation from an n-best list based on the reference simplification.

we see an even larger gain by Moses+Del with a difference of 0.07 BLEU.

For completeness, we also trained Moses+Del on the same 30K sentences used to train the T3 system.[5] Using this training data, Moses+Del achieved a BLEU score of 0.5952. This is less than the score achieved when using the full training data, but is significantly better than T3 and still represents a small improvement over *none*.

Table 6 shows example simplifications made by Moses+Del. In many of the examples we see phrasal deletion during the simplification process. The output also contains a number of reasonable lexical changes, for example in *a*, *d* and *e*. Example *b* contains reordering and *e* shows an example of a split being performed where the normal sentence is turned into two simplified sentences. This is not uncommon in the data, but can be challenging to model for current syntactic approaches. The examples also highlight some of the common issues with the approach. Examples *a* and *f* are not grammatically correct and the simplification in *f* does not preserve the original meaning of the text. As an aside, the normal sentence of example *d* also contains an omission error following "as" due to preprocessing of the data, resulting from ill-formed xml in the articles.

5.3 Oracle

In the previous section, we looked at the performance of the systems based on the best translations suggested by the systems. For many approaches, we can also generate an n-best list of possible translations. We examined the simplifications in this n-best list to measure the potential benefit of reranking techniques, which have proved successful in many NLP applications (Och et al., 2004; Ge and Mooney, 2006), and to understand how well the underlying model captures the phenomena exhibited in the data. For both of the phrase-based approaches, we generated an n-best list of size 1000 for each sentence in the test set. Using these n-best lists, we generated an "oracle" simplification of the test set by greedily selecting for each test sentence the simplification in the n-best list with the best sentence-level BLEU score.

Table 7 shows the BLEU scores for the original system output and the system's oracle output. In all cases, there is a large difference between the system's current output and the oracle output, suggesting that utilizing some reranking technique could be useful. Also, we again see the benefit of the phrasal deletion rules. The addition of the phrasal deletion rule gives the system an additional dimension of flexibility, resulting in a more varied n-best list and an overall higher oracle BLEU score.

6 Conclusions and Future Work

In this paper, we have explored a variety of approaches for learning to simplify sentences from Wikipedia. In contrast to prior work in the related field of sentence compression where deletion plays the dominant role, the simplification task we examined has the full range of text-to-text operations including lexical changes, reordering, insertions and deletions.

We implemented a modified phrase-based simplification approach that incorporates phrasal deletion. Our approach performs significantly better than two different text compression approaches, including T3, and better than previous approaches on a similar data set (Zhu et al., 2010). We also showed

[5]To be completely consistent with T3, we used the first 29,700 pairs for training and the last 300 for parameter tuning.

a.	normal:	*Critical reception* for The Wild has been negative.
	simplified:	*Reviews* for The Wild has been negative.
b.	normal:	Bauska is a town in Bauska county , in the *Zemgale* region of *southern Latvia* .
	simplified:	Bauska is a town in Bauska county , in the region of *Zemgale* .
c.	normal:	LaBalme is a commune *in the Ain department in eastern France* .
	simplified:	LaBalme is a commune .
d.	normal:	Shadow of the Colossus , *released in Japan as* , is a Japanese-developed action-adventure video game *developed and published* by Sony computer entertainment for the Playstation 2.
	simplified:	Shadow of the Colossus is a Japanese-developed action-adventure video game *made* by Sony computer entertainment for the Playstation 2.
e.	normal:	Nicolas Anelka is a French *footballer who currently* plays as a striker for Chelsea *in the English premier league* .
	simplified:	Nicolas Anelka is a French *football player* . *He* plays for Chelsea .
f.	normal:	*Each* edge of *a tesseract is* of the same length.
	simplified:	*Same* edge of the same length.

Table 6: Example simplifications. "normal" is the the unsimplified input sentence and "simplified" the simplification made by Moses+Del.

that the incorporation of phrasal deletion into the simplification process results in statistically significant improvements over a traditional phrase-based approach.

While we obtained positive results using a phrase-based approach, we still believe that incorporating some additional hierarchical structure will help the simplification process, particularly since one of the goals of simplification is to reduce the grammatical complexity of the sentence. Also, as seen in some of the examples above, the phrase-based model can produce output that is not grammatically correct. Though T3 did not perform well, many other syntax-based models exists that have been successful in machine translation.

There are a number of research questions motivated by this work in related areas including the scalability of discriminative trained rule sets, the impact of the language model training source (simple vs. normal English), document-level simplification and applications of text simplification. Our hope is that this new simplification task will spur a variety of related research inquiries.

Acknowledgments

We'd like to thank Dan Feblowitz for his insights and discussions, and for generating the results for the K & M implementation.

References

Regina Barzilay and Noemie Elhadad. 2003. Sentence alignment for monolingual comparable corpora. In *Proceedings of EMNLP*.

Yvonne Canning, John Tait, Jackie Archibald, and Ros Crawley. 2000. Cohesive generation of syntactically simplified newspaper text. In *Proceedings of TSD*.

John Carroll, Gido Minnen, Yvonne Canning, Siobhan Devlin, and John Tait. 1998. Practical simplification of English newspaper text to assist aphasic readers. In *Proceedings of AAAI Workshop on Integrating AI and Assistive Technology*.

Raman Chandrasekar and Bangalore Srinivas. 1997. Automatic induction of rules for text simplification. In *Knowledge Based Systems*.

Yu Chen, Martin Kay, and Andreas Eisele. 2009. Intersecting multilingual data for faster and better statistical translations. In *Proceedings of HLT/NAACL*.

David Chiang. 2010. Learning to translate with source and target syntax. In *Proceedings of ACL*.

James Clarke and Mirella Lapata. 2006. Models for sentence compression: A comparison across domains, training requirements and evaluation measures. In *Proceedings of ACL*.

Trevor Cohn and Mirella Lapata. 2009. Sentence compression as tree transduction. *Journal of Artificial Intelligence Research*.

Will Coster and David Kauchak. 2011. Simple English Wikipedia: A new simplification task. In *Proceedings of ACL (Short Paper)*.

Lijun Feng. 2008. Text simplification: A survey. CUNY Technical Report.

Michel Galley and Kathleen McKeown. 2007. Lexicalized Markov grammars for sentence compression. In *Proceedings of HLT/NAACL*.

Ruifang Ge and Raymond Mooney. 2006. Discriminative reranking for semantic parsing. In *Proceedings of COLING*.

Dan Klein and Christopher Manning. 2003. Accurate unlexicalized parsing. In *Proceedings of ACL*.

Kevin Knight and Daniel Marcu. 2002. Summarization beyond sentence extraction: A probabilistic approach to sentence compression. *Artificial Intelligence*.

Philipp Koehn, Hieu Hoang, Alexandra Birch, Chris Callison-Burch, Marcello Federico, Nicola Bertoldi, Brooke Cowan, Wade Shen, Christine Moran, Richard Zens, Chris Dyer, Ondrej Bojar, Alexandra Constantin, and Evan Herbst. 2007. Moses: Open source toolkit for statistical machine translation. In *Proceedings of ACL*.

Philipp Koehn. 2004. Statistical significance tests for machine translation evaluation. In *Proceedings of EMNLP*.

Ryan McDonald. 2006. Discriminative sentence compression with soft syntactic evidence. In *Proceedings of EACL*.

Makoto Miwa, Rune Saetre, Yusuke Miyao, and Jun'ichi Tsujii. 2010. Entity-focused sentence simplication for relation extraction. In *Proceedings of COLING*.

Courtney Napoles and Mark Dredze. 2010. Learning simple Wikipedia: A cogitation in ascertaining abecedarian language. In *Proceedings of HLT/NAACL Workshop on Computation Linguistics and Writing*.

Rani Nelken and Stuart Shieber. 2006. Towards robust context-sensitive sentence alignment for monolingual corpora. In *Proceedings of AMTA*.

Tadashi Nomoto. 2007. Discriminative sentence compression with conditional random fields. In *Information Processing and Management*.

Tadashi Nomoto. 2008. A generic sentence trimmer with CRFs. In *Proceedings of HLT/NAACL*.

Tadashi Nomoto. 2009. A comparison of model free versus model intensive approaches to sentence compression. In *Proceedings of EMNLP*.

F.J. Och and H. Ney. 2000. Improved statistical alignment models. In *Proceedings of ACL*.

Franz Josef Och and Hermann Ney. 2003. A systematic comparison of various statistical alignment models. *Computational Linguistics*, 29(1):19–51.

Franz Josef Och, Kenji Yamada, Stanford U, Alex Fraser, Daniel Gildea, and Viren Jain. 2004. A smorgasbord of features for statistical machine translation. In *Proceedings of HLT/NAACL*.

Kishore Papineni, Salim Roukos, Todd Ward, and Wei-Jing Zhu. 2002. BLEU: a method for automatic evaluation of machine translation. In *Proceedings of ACL*.

Jenine Turner and Eugene Charniak. 2005. Supervised and unsupervised learning for sentence compression. In *Proceedings of ACL*.

David Vickrey and Daphne Koller. 2008. Sentence simplification for semantic role labeling. In *Proceedings of ACL*.

S. Wubben, A. van den Bosch, and E. Krahmer. 2010. Paraphrase generation as monolingual translation: Data and evaluation. In *Proceedings of the International Workshop on Natural Language Generation*.

Elif Yamangil and Rani Nelken. 2008. Mining Wikipedia revision histories for improving sentence compression. In *ACL*.

Mark Yatskar, Bo Pang, Critian Danescu-Niculescu-Mizil, and Lillian Lee. 2010. For the sake of simplicity: Unsupervised extraction of lexical simplifications from Wikipedia. In *Proceedings of HLT/NAACL (Short Paper)*.

Zhemin Zhu, Delphine Bernhard, and Iryna Gurevych. 2010. A monolingual tree-based translation model for sentence simplification. In *Proceedings of COLING*.

Web-based validation for contextual targeted paraphrasing

Houda Bouamor
LIMSI-CNRS
Univ. Paris Sud
hbouamor@limsi.fr

Aurélien Max
LIMSI-CNRS
Univ. Paris Sud
amax@limsi.fr

Gabriel Illouz
LIMSI-CNRS
Univ. Paris Sud
gabrieli@limsi.fr

Anne Vilnat
LIMSI-CNRS
Univ. Paris Sud
anne@limsi.fr

Abstract

In this work, we present a scenario where contextual targeted paraphrasing of sub-sentential phrases is performed automatically to support the task of text revision. Candidate paraphrases are obtained from a preexisting repertoire and validated in the context of the original sentence using information derived from the Web. We report on experiments on French, where the original sentences to be rewritten are taken from a rewriting memory automatically extracted from the edit history of Wikipedia.

1 Introduction

There are many instances where it is reasonable to expect machines to produce text automatically. Traditionally, this was tackled as a concept-to-text realization problem. However, such needs apply sometimes to cases where a new text should be derived from some existing texts, an instance of text-to-text generation. The general idea is not anymore to produce a text from data, but to transform a text so as to ensure that it has desirable properties appropriate for some intended application (Zhao et al., 2009). For example, one may want a text to be shorter (Cohn and Lapata, 2008), tailored to some reader profile (Zhu et al., 2010), compliant with some specific norms (Max, 2004), or more adapted for subsequent machine processing tasks (Chandrasekar et al., 1996). The generation process must produce a text having a meaning which is compatible with the definition of the task at hand (e.g. strict paraphrasing for document normalization, relaxed paraphrasing for text simplification), while ensuring that it remains grammatically correct. Its complexity, compared with concept-to-text generation, mostly stems from the fact that the semantic relationship between the original text and the new one is more difficult to control, as the mapping from one text to another is very dependent on the rewriting context. The wide variety of techniques for acquiring phrasal paraphrases, which can subsequently be used by text paraphrasing techniques (Madnani and Dorr, 2010), the inherent polysemy of such linguistic units and the pragmatic constraints on their uses make it impossible to ensure that potential paraphrase pairs will be substitutable in any context, an observation which was already made at a lexical level (Zhao et al., 2007). Hence, automatic contextual validation of candidate rewritings is a fundamental issue for text paraphrasing with phrasal units.

In this article, we tackle the problem of what we call *targeted paraphrasing*, defined as the rewriting of a subpart of a sentence, as in e.g. (Resnik et al., 2010) where it is applied to making parts of sentences easier to translate automatically. While this problem is simpler than full sentence rewriting, its study is justified as it should be handled correctly for the more complex task to be successful. Moreover, being simpler, it offers evaluation scenarios which make the performance on the task easier to assess. Our particular experiments here aim to assist a Wikipedia contributor in revising a text to improve its quality. For this, we use a collection of phrases that have been rewritten in Wikipedia, and test the substitutability of paraphrases coming from a repertoire of sub-sentential paraphrases acquired from different sources. We thus consider that preexisting repertoires of sub-sentential paraphrase pairs are available, and that each potential candidate has to be tested in the specific context of the desired rewriting. Due to the large variety of potential phrases and their associated known paraphrases, we do not rely on precomputed models of substitutability, but rather build them on-the-fly using information derived from web queries.[1]

This article is organized as follows. In section 2, we first describe the task of text revision, where a subpart of a sentence is rewritten, as an instance of targeted paraphrasing. Section 3 presents previous works on the acquisition of sub-sentential paraphrases and describes the knowledge sources that we have used in this work. We then describe in section 4 how we estimate models of phrase substitution in context by exploiting information coming from the web. We present our experiments and their results in section 5, and finally discuss our current results and future work in section 6.

2 Targeted paraphrasing for text revision

One of the important processes of text revision is the rewording of parts of sentences. Some rewordings are not intended to alter meaning significantly, but rather to make text more coherent and easier to comprehend. Those instances which express close meanings are sub-sentential paraphrases: in their simpler form, they can involve synonym substitution, but they can involve more complex deeper lexical-syntactic transformations.

Such rephrasings are commonly found in recordings of text revisions, which now exist in large quantities in the collaborative editing model of Wikipedia. In fact, revision histories of the encyclopedia contain a significant amount of sub-sentential paraphrases, as shown by the study of (Dutrey et al., 2011). This study also reports that there is an important variety of rephrasing phenomena, as illustrated by the difficulty of reaching a good identification coverage using a rule-based term variant identification engine.

The use of automatic targeted paraphrasing as an authoring aid has been illustrated by the work of Max and Zock (2008), in which writers are presented with potential paraphrases of sub-sentential fragments that they wish to reword. The automatic paraphrasing technique used is a contextual variant of bilingual translation pivoting (Bannard and Callison-Burch, 2005). It has also been proposed to externalize various text editing tasks, including proofreading, by having crowdsourcing functions on text directly from word processors (Bernstein et al., 2010).

Text improvements may also be more specifically targeted for automatic applications. In the work by Resnik *et al.* (2010), rephrasings for specific phrases are acquired through crowdsourcing. Difficult-to-translate phrases in the source text are first identified, and monolingual contributors are asked to provide rephrasings in context. Collected rephrasings can then be used as input for a Machine Translation system, which can positively exploit the increased variety in expression to produce more confident translations for better estimated source units (Schroeder et al., 2009).[2] For instance, the phrase in bold in the sentence *The number of people* ***known to have died*** *has now reached 358* can be rewritten as 1) *who died*, 2) *identified to have died* and 3) *known to have passed away*. All such rephrasings are grammatically correct, the first one being significantly shorter, and they all convey a meaning which is reasonably close to the original wording.

The task of rewriting complete sentences has also been addressed in various works (e.g. (Barzilay and Lee, 2003; Quirk et al., 2004; Zhao et al., 2010)). It poses, however, numerous other challenges, in particular regarding how it could be correctly evaluated. Human judgments of whole sentence transformations are complex and intra- and inter-judge coherence is difficult to attain with hypotheses of comparable quality. Using sentential paraphrases to support a given task (e.g. providing alternative reference translations for optimizing Statistical Machine Translation systems (Madnani et al., 2008))

[1] Note that using the web may not always be appropriate, or that at least it should be used in a different way than what we propose in this article, in particular in cases where the desired properties of the rewritten text are better described in controlled corpora.

[2] It is to be noted that, in the scenario presented in (Resnik et al., 2010), monolingual contributors cannot predict how useful their rewritings will be to the underlying Machine Translation engine used.

can be seen as a proxy for extrinsic evaluation of the quality of paraphrases, but it is not clear from published results that improvements on the task are clearly correlated with the quality of the produced paraphrases. Lastly, automatic metrics have been proposed for evaluating the grammaticality of sentences (e.g. (Mutton et al., 2007)). Automatic evaluation of sentential paraphrases has not produced any consensual results so far, as they do not integrate task-specific considerations and can be strongly biased towards some paraphrasing techniques.

In this work, we tackle the comparatively more modest task of sub-sentential paraphrasing applied to text revision. In order to use an unbiased task, we use a corpus of naturally-occurring rewritings from an authoring memory of Wikipedia articles. We use the WICOPACO corpus (Max and Wisniewski, 2010), a collection of local rephrasings from the edit history of Wikipedia which contains instances of lexical, syntactical and semantic rephrasings (Dutrey et al., 2011), the latter type being illustrated by the following example:

Ce vers de Nuit rhénane d'Apollinaire ***[qui paraît presque sans structure rythmique → dont la césure est comme masquée]****...* [3]

The appropriateness of this corpus for our work is twofold: first, the fact that it contains naturally-occurring rewritings provides us with an interesting source of text spans in context which have been rewritten. Moreover, for those instances where the meaning after rewriting was not significantly altered, it provides us with at least one candidate rewriting that should be considered as a correct paraphrase, which can be useful for training validation algorithms.

3 Automatic sub-sentential paraphrase acquisition and generation

The acquisition of paraphrases, and in particular of sub-sentential paraphrases and paraphrase patterns, has attracted a lot of works with the advent of data-intensive Natural Language Processing (Madnani and Dorr, 2010). The techniques proposed have a strong relationship to the type of text corpus used for acquisition, mainly:

- pairs of sentential paraphrases (**monolingual parallel corpora**) allow for a good precision but evidently a low recall (e.g. (Barzilay and McKeown, 2001; Pang et al., 2003; Cohn et al., 2008; Bouamor et al., 2011))
- pairs of bilingual sentences (**bilingual parallel corpora**) allow for a comparatively better recall (e.g. (Bannard and Callison-Burch, 2005; Kok and Brockett, 2010))
- pairs of related sentences (**monolingual comparable corpora**) allow for even higher recall but possibly lower precision (e.g. (Barzilay and Lee, 2003; Li et al., 2005; Bhagat and Ravichandran, 2008; Deléger and Zweigenbaum, 2009)

Although the precision of such techniques can in some cases be formulated with regards to a predefined reference set (Cohn et al., 2008), it should more generally be assessed in the specific context of some use of the paraphrase pair. This refers to the problem of *substituability in context* (e.g. (Connor and Roth, 2007; Zhao et al., 2007)), which is a well studied field at the lexical level and the object of evaluation campains (McCarthy and Navigli, 2009). Contextual phrase substitution poses the additional challenge that phrases are rarer than words, so that building contextual and grammatical models to ensure that the generated rephrasings are both semantically compatible and grammatical is more complicated (e.g. (Callison-Burch, 2008)).

The present work does not aim to present any original technique for paraphrase acquisition, but rather focusses on the task of sub-sentential paraphrase validation in context. We thus resort to some existing repertoire of phrasal paraphrase pairs. As explained in section 2, we use the WICOPACO corpus as a source of sub-sentential paraphrases: the phrase after rewriting can thus be used as a potential paraphrase in context.[4] To obtain other candidates of various quality, we used two knowledge sources. The first uses automatic pivot translation (Bannard and Callison-Burch, 2005), where a state-of-the-art

[3] *This verse from Apollinaire's Nuit Rhénane* ***[which seems almost without rhythmic structure → whose cesura is as if hidden]****...*

[4] Note, however, that in our experiments we will ask our human judges to assess anew its paraphrasing status in context.

general-purpose Statistical Machine Translation system is used in a two-way translation. The second uses manual acquisition of paraphrase candidates. Web-based acquisition of this type of knowledge has already been done before (Chklovski, 2005; España Bonet et al., 2009), and could be done by crowdsourcing, a technique growing in popularity in recent years. We have instead formulated manual acquisition as a web-based game. Players can take parts in two parts of the game, illustrated on Figure 3.

First, players propose sub-sentential paraphrases in context for selected text spans in web documents (top of Figure 3), and then raters can take part in assessing paraphrases proposed by other players (bottom of Figure 3). In order to avoid any bias, players cannot evaluate games in which they played. Evaluation is sped up by using a compact word lattice view for eliciting human judgments, built using the syntactic fusion algorithm of (Pang et al., 2003). Data acquisition was done in French to remain coherent with our experiments on the French corpus of WiCoPaCo, and both players and raters were native speakers. An important point is that in our experiments the context of acquisition and of evaluation were different: players were asked to generate paraphrases in contexts that are different from those of the WiCoPaCo corpus used for evaluation. To this end, web snippets were automatically retrieved for the various phrases of our dataset without contexts, so that sentences from the Web (but not from Wikipedia) were used for manual paraphrase acquisition. This allows us to simulate the availability of a preexisting repertoire of (contextless) sub-sentential paraphrases, and to assess the performance of our contextual validation techniques on a possibly incompatible context.

4 Web-based contextual validation

Given a repertoire of potential phrasal paraphrases and a context for a naturally-occurring rewriting, our task consists in deciding automatically which potential paraphrases can be substituted with good confidence for the original phrase. A concrete instantiation of it could correspond to the proposal of Max and Zock (2008), where such candidate rephrasings could be presented in order of decreasing suitability to a word processor user, possibly during the revision of a Wikipedia article.

The specific nature of the text units that we are dealing with calls for a careful treatment: in the general scenario, it is unlikely that any supervised corpus would contain enough information for appropriate modeling of the substituability in context decision. It is therefore tempting to consider using the Web as the largest available information source, in spite of several of its known limitations, including that data can be of varying quality. It has however been shown that a large range of NLP applications can be improved by exploiting n-gram counts from the Web (using Web document counts as a proxy) (Lapata and Keller, 2005).

Paraphrase identification has been addressed previously, both using features computed from an offline corpus (Brockett and Dolan, 2005) and features computed from Web queries (Zhao et al., 2007). However, to our knowledge previous work exploiting information from the Web was limited to the identification of lexical paraphrases. Although the probability of finding phrase occurrences significantly increases by considering the Web, some phrases are still very rare or not present in search engine indexes.

As in (Brockett and Dolan, 2005), we tackle our paraphrase identification task as one of monolingual classification. More precisely, considering an original phrase p within the context of sentence s, we seek to determine whether a candidate paraphrase p' would be a grammatical paraphrase of p within the context of s. We make use of a Support Vector Machine (SVM) classifier which exploits the features described in the remainder of this section.

Edit distance model score Surface similarity on phrase pairs can be a good indicator that they share semantic content. In order to account for the cost of transforming one string into the other, rather than simply counting common words, we use the score produced by the Translation Edit Rate metric (Snover et al., 2010). Furthermore, we perform this computation on strings of lemmas rather than surface forms:[5]

[5]Note that because we computed the TER metric on French strings, stemming and semantic matching through WordNet were not activated.

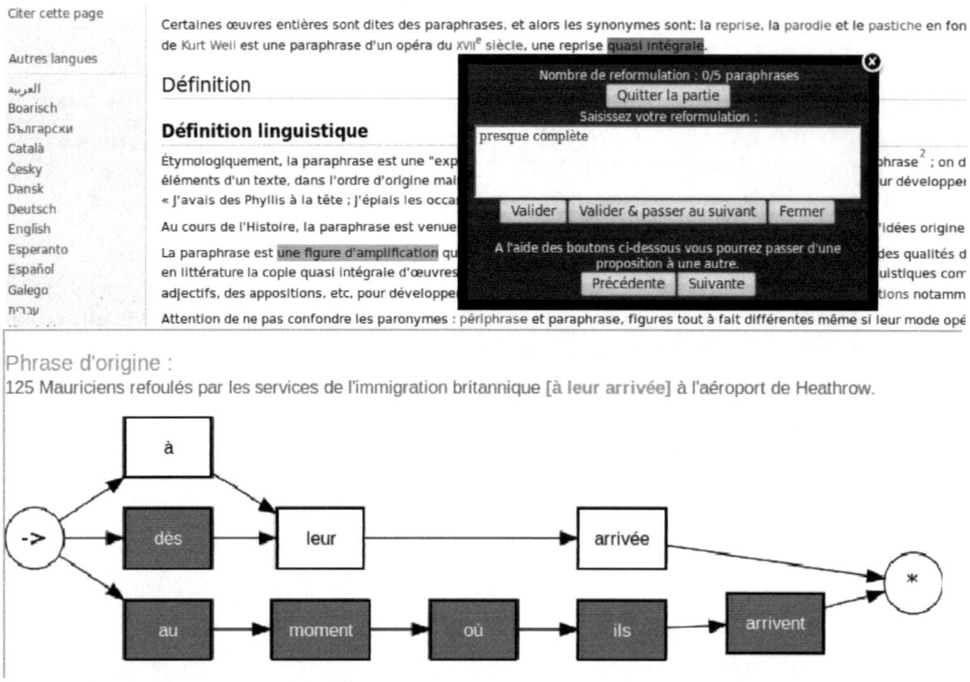

Figure 1: Interface of our web-based game for paraphrase acquisition and evaluation. On the top, players reformulate all text spans highlighted by the game creator on any webpage (a Wikipedia article on the example). On the bottom, raters evaluate paraphrases proposed by sets of players using a compact word-lattice view. Note that in its standard definition, the game attributes higher scores to paraphrase candidates that are highly rated and rarer.

$$h_{edit} = \text{TER}(Lem_{orig}, Lem_{para}) \quad (1)$$

Note that this model is not derived from information from the Web, in contrast to all the models described next.

Language model score The likelihood of a sentence can be a good indicator of its grammaticality (Mutton, 2006). Language model probabilities can now be obtained from Web counts. In our experiments, we used the Microsoft Web N-gram Service[6] for research (Wang et al., 2010) to obtain log likelihood scores for text units.[7] However, this score is certainly not sufficient as it does not take the original wording into account. We therefore used a ratio of the language model score of the paraphrased sentence with the language model score of the original sentence, after normalization by sentence length of the language model scores (Onishi et al., 2010):

$$h_{LM\_ratio} = \frac{LM(para)}{LM(orig)} = \frac{lm(para)^{1/length(para)}}{lm(orig)^{1/length(orig)}} \quad (2)$$

Contextless thematic model scores Cooccurring words are used in distributional semantics to account for common meanings of words. We build vector representations of cooccurrences for both the original phrase p and its paraphrase p'. Our contextless thematic model is built in the following fashion: we query a search engine to retrieve the top N document snippets for phrase p. We then count frequencies for all content words in these snippets, and keep the set W of words appearing more than a fraction of N. We then build a vector T (thematic profile) of dimension $|W|$ where values are computed by the following formula:

$$T_{orig}^{nocont}[w] = \frac{count(p, w)}{count(p)} \quad (3)$$

[6] `http://research.microsoft.com/en-us/collaboration/focus/cs/web-ngram.aspx`

[7] Note that in order to query on French text, we had to remove all diacritics for the service to behave correctly, independently of encodings: careful examination of ranked hypotheses showed that this trick allowed us to obtain results coherent with expectations.

where $count(x)$ correspond to the number of documents containing a given exact phrase or word according to the search engine used and $count(x, y)$ correspond to the number of documents containing simultaneously both. We then compute the same thematic profile for the paraphrase p', using only the subset of words W:

$$T_{para}^{nocont}[w] = \frac{count(p', w)}{count(p)} \quad (4)$$

Finally, we compute a similarity between the two profiles by taking the cosinus between their two vectors:

$$h_{them}^{nocont} = \frac{T_{orig}^{nocont} \cdot T_{para}^{nocont}}{||T_{orig}^{nocont}|| * ||T_{para}^{nocont}||} \quad (5)$$

In all our experiments, we used the Yahoo! Search BOSS[8] Web service for obtaining Web counts and retrieving snippets. Assuming that the distribution of words in W is not biased by the result ordering of the search engine, our model measures some similarity between the most cooccurring content words with p and the same words with p'.

Context-aware thematic model scores Our context-aware thematic model takes into account the words of sentence s in which the substitution of p with p' is attempted. We now consider the set of content words from s (s being the part of the sentence without phrase p) in lieu of the previous set of cooccurring words W, and compute the same profile vectors and similarity between that of the original sentence and that of the paraphrased sentence:

$$h_{them}^{cont} = \frac{T_{orig}^{cont} \cdot T_{para}^{cont}}{||T_{orig}^{cont}|| * ||T_{para}^{cont}||} \quad (6)$$

However, words from s might not be strongly cooccurring with p. In order to increase the likelihood of finding thematically related words, we also build an extended context model, $h_{them}^{extcont}$ where content words from s are supplemented with their most cooccurring words. This is done using the same procedure as that previously used for finding content words cooccurring with p.

[8]http://developer.yahoo.com/search/boss/

5 Experiments

In this section we report on experiments conducted to assess the performance of our proposed approach for validating candidate sub-sentential paraphrases using information from the Web.

5.1 Data used

We randomly extracted 150 original sentences in French and their rewritings from the WICOPACO corpus which were marked as paraphrases. Of those, we kept 100 for our training corpus and the remaining 50 for testing. The number of original phrases of each length is reported on Figure 2.

phrase length	1	2	3	4	5	6	7	8
original phrases	0	3	29	8	6	2	2	0
paraphrases	39	64	74	36	21	10	5	1

Figure 2: Distribution of number of phrases per phrase length in tokens for the test corpus

For each original sentence, we collected 5 candidate paraphrases to simulate the fact that we had a repertoire of paraphrases with the required entries:[9]

- WICOPACO: the original paraphrase from the WICOPACO corpus;
- GAME: two candidate paraphrases from users of our Web-based game;
- PIVOT$_{ES}$ and PIVOT$_{ZH}$: two candidate paraphrases obtained by translation by pivot, using the Google Translate[10] online SMT system and one language close to French as pivot (Spanish), and another one more distant (Chinese).

We then presented the original sentence and its 5 paraphrases (in random order) to two judges. Four native speakers took part in our experiments: they all took part in the data collection for one half of the sentences of the training and test corpora and to the evaluation of paraphrases for the other half. For the annotation with two classes (paraphrase vs. not paraphrase), we obtain as inter-judge agreement[11] a

[9]Note that, as a consequence, we did not carry any experiment related to the recall of any technique here.

[10]http://translate.google.com

[11]We used R (http://www.r-project.org) to compute this Cohen's κ value.

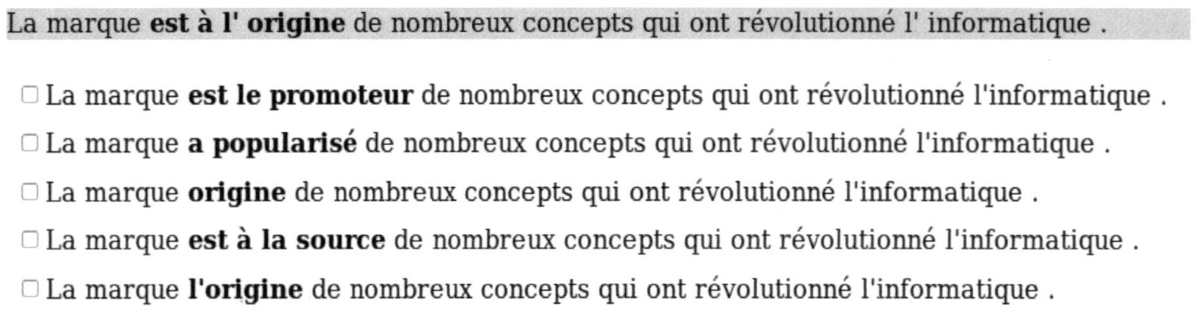

Figure 3: Example of an original sentence and its 5 associated candidate paraphrases. The phrase in bold from the original sentence (*The brand* ***is at the origin*** *of many concepts that have revolutionized computing.*) is paraphrased as *est le promoteur* (*is the promoter*), *a popularisé* (*popularized*), *origine* (*origin*), *est à la source* (*is the source*), and *l'origine* (*the origin*).

value of $\kappa = 0.65$, corresponding to a *substantial* agreement according to the literature. An example of the interface used is provided in Figure 3.

We considered that our technique could not propose reliable results when web phrase counts were too low. From the distribution of counts of phrases and paraphrases from our training set (see Figure 4), we empirically chose a threshold of 10 for the minimum count of any phrase. Our corpus was consequently reduced from 750=150*5 to 434 examples for the training corpus, and from 250=50*5 to 215 for the test corpus.

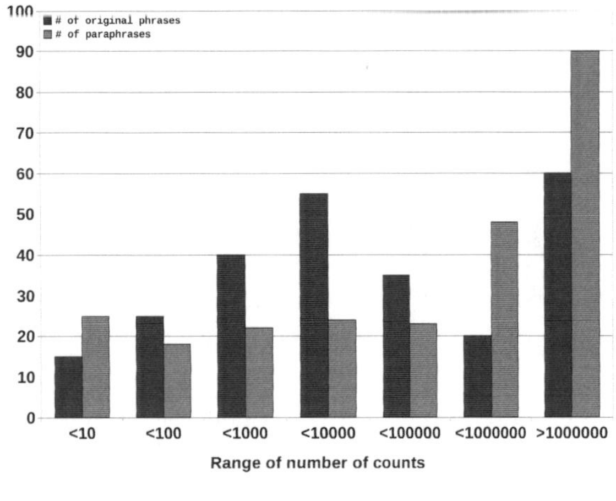

Figure 4: Number of phrases and paraphrases per web count range

Results will be reported for three conditions:

- **Possible**: the gold standard for instances where at least one of the judges indicated "paraphrases" records the pair as a paraphrase. In this condition, the test set has 116 instances that are paraphrases and 99 that are not.
- **Sure**: the gold standard for instances where not all judges indicated "paraphrases" records the pair as not paraphrase. In this condition, the test set has 76 instances that are paraphrases and 139 that are not.
- **Surer**: only those instances where both judges agree are recorded. This reduces our training and test set to respectively 287 and 175 examples. Thus, results on this subcorpora will not be directly comparable with the other results. In this condition, the test set has 76 instances that are paraphrases and 99 that are not.

5.2 Baseline techniques

Web-count based baselines We used two baselines based on simple Web counts. The first one, WEBLM, considers a candidate sentence a paraphrase of the original sentence whenever its Web language model score is higher than that of the original phrase. The second one, BOUNDLM, considers a sentence as a paraphrase whenever the counts for the bigrams crossing the left and right boundary of the sub-sentential paraphrase is higher than 10.

Syntactic dependency baseline When rewriting a subpart of a sentence, the fact that syntactic dependencies between the rewritten phrase and its context are the same than those of the original phrase and the same context can provide some information about the grammatical and semantic substituability of the two phrases (Zhao et al., 2007; Max and Zock, 2008). We thus build syntactic dependencies for both the original and rewritten sentence, using the French version (Candito et al., 2010) of the Berkeley probabilistic parser (Petrov and Klein, 2007), and consider the subset of dependencies for the two sentences that exist between a word inside the phrase under focus and a word outside it (Dep_{orig} and Dep_{para}). Our CONTDEP baseline considers a sentence as a paraphrase iff $Dep_{para} = Dep_{orig}$.

5.3 Evaluation results

We used the models described in Section 4 to build a SVM classifier using the LIBSVM package (Chang and Lin, 2001). Accuracy results are reported on Figure 5.

	WEBLM	BOUNDLM	CONTDEP	CLASSIFIER
POSSIBLE	**62.79**	54.88	48.53	57.67
SURE	68.37	36.27	51.90	**70.69**
SURER	56.79	51.41	42.69	**62.85**

Figure 5: Accuracy results for the three baselines and our classifier on the test set for the three conditions. Note that the SURER condition cannot be directly compared with the other two as the number of training and test examples are not the same.

The first notable observation is that our task is not surprisingly a difficult one. The best performance achieved is an accuracy of 70.69 with our system in the SURE condition. There are, however, some important variations across conditions, with a result as low as 57.67 for our system in the POSSIBLE condition (recall that in this condition candidates are considered paraphrases when only one of the two judges considered it a paraphrase, i.e. when the two judges disagreed).

Overall, the WEBLM baseline and our system appear as stronger than the two other baselines. The two lower baselines, BOUNDLM and CONTDEP, attempt to model local grammatical constraints, which are not surprisingly not sufficient for paraphrase identification. WEBLM is comparatively a much more competitive baseline, but its accuracy in the SURER condition is not very strong. As this latter condition considers only consensual judgements for the two judges, we can hypothesize that the interpretation of its results is more reliable. In this condition, our system obtains the best performance, with a +6.06 advantage over WEBLM. As found in other works (e.g. (Bannard and Callison-Burch, 2005)), using language models for paraphrase validation is not sufficient as it cannot model meaning preservation, and our results show that this is also true even when counts are estimated from the Web. Using a ratio of normalized LM scores may have improved the situation a bit.[12]

	WICOPACO	GAMERS	PIVOT_{ES}	PIVOT_{ZH}
POSSIBLE	**89.33**	67.00	47.33	20.66
SURE	**64.00**	44.50	31.33	10.66
SURER	**86.03**	57.34	37.71	12.60

Figure 6: Paraphrase accuracy of our different paraphrase acquisition methods for the three conditions.

Lastly, we report in Figure 6 the paraphrase accuracy of each individual acquisition technique (i.e. source of paraphrases from the preexisting repertoire). The original rewritting from WICOPACO obtains not surprisingly a very high paraphrase accuracy, in particular in the POSSIBLE and SURER conditions. Paraphrases obtained through our Web-based game have an acceptable accuracy: the numbers confirm that paraphrase pairs are highly context-dependent, because the pairs which were likely to be paraphrases in the context of the game are not necessarily so in a different context. This, of course, may be due to a number of reasons that we will have to investigate. Lastly, there is a significant drop in accuracy for the automatic pivot paraphrasers, but pivoting through Spanish obtained, not suprisingly again, a much better performance than pivoting through Chinese.

6 Discussion and future work

We have presented an approach to the task of targeted paraphrasing in the context of text revision, a scenario which was supported by naturally-occurring data from the rephrasing memory of Wikipedia. Our framework takes a repertoire of existing sub-sentential paraphrases, coming from pos-

[12] A possible explanation for the relative good performance of WEBLM may lie in the fact that our two automatic paraphrasers using Google Translate as a pivot translation engine tend to produce strings that are very likely according to the language models used by the translation system, which we assume to be very comparable to those that were used in our experiments.

sibly any source including manual acquisition, and validates all candidate paraphrases using information from the Web. Our experiments have shown that the current version of our classifier outperforms several baselines when considering paraphrases with consensual judgements in the gold standard reference.

Although our initial experiments are positive, we believe that they can be improved in a number of ways. We intend to broaden our exploration of the various characteristics at play. We will try more features, including e.g. a model of syntactic dependencies derived from the Web, and extend our work to new languages. We will also attempt to analyze more precisely our results to identify problematic cases, some of which could turn to be almost impossible to model without resorting to world knowledge, which was beyond our attempted modeling. Finally, we will also be interested in considering the applicability of this approach as a framework for the evaluation of paraphrase acquisition techniques.

Acknowledgments

This work was partly supported by ANR project Trace (ANR-09-CORD-023). The authors would like to thank the anonymous reviewers for their helpful questions and comments.

References

Colin Bannard and Chris Callison-Burch. 2005. Paraphrasing with bilingual parallel corpora. In *Proceedings of ACL*, Ann Arbor, USA.

Regina Barzilay and Lillian Lee. 2003. Learning to paraphrase: an unsupervised approach using multiple-sequence alignment. In *Proceedings of NAACL-HLT*, Edmonton, Canada.

Regina Barzilay and Kathleen McKeown. 2001. Extracting paraphrases from a parallel corpus. In *Proceedings of ACL*, Toulouse, France.

Michael S. Bernstein, Greg Little, Robert C. Miller, Björn Hartmann, Mark S. Ackerman, David R. Karger, David Crowell, and Katrina Panovich. 2010. Soylent: a word processor with a crowd inside. In *Proceedings of the ACM symposium on User interface software and technology*.

Rahul Bhagat and Deepak Ravichandran. 2008. Large scale acquisition of paraphrases for learning surface patterns. In *Proceedings of ACL-HLT*, Columbus, USA.

Houda Bouamor, Aurélien Max, and Anne Vilnat. 2011. Monolingual alignment by edit rate computation on sentential paraphrase pairs. In *Proceedings of ACL, Short Papers session*, Portland, USA.

Chris Brockett and William B. Dolan. 2005. Support vector machines for paraphrase identification and corpus construction. In *Proceedings of The 3rd International Workshop on Paraphrasing IWP*, Jeju Island, South Korea.

Chris Callison-Burch. 2008. Syntactic constraints on paraphrases extracted from parallel corpora. In *Proceedings of EMNLP*, Hawai, USA.

Marie Candito, Benoît Crabbé, and Pascal Denis. 2010. Statistical french dependency parsing: treebank conversion and first results. In *Proceedings of LREC*, Valletta, Malta.

R. Chandrasekar, Christine Doran, and B. Srinivas. 1996. Motivations and methods for text simplification. In *Proceedings of COLING*, Copenhagen, Denmark.

Chih-Chung Chang and Chih-Jen Lin, 2001. *LIBSVM: a library for support vector machines*. Software available at `http://www.csie.ntu.edu.tw/~cjlin/libsvm`.

Timothy Chklovski. 2005. Collecting paraphrase corpora from volunteer contributors. In *Proceedings of KCAP 2005*, Banff, Canada.

Trevor Cohn and Mirella Lapata. 2008. Sentence compression beyond word deletion. In *Proceedings of COLING*, Manchester, UK.

Trevor Cohn, Chris Callison-Burch, and Mirella Lapata. 2008. Constructing corpora for the development and evaluation of paraphrase systems. *Comput. Linguist.*, 34(4):597–614.

Michael Connor and Dan Roth. 2007. Context sensitive paraphrasing with a global unsupervised classifier. In *Proceedings of ECML*, Warsaw, Poland.

Louise Deléger and Pierre Zweigenbaum. 2009. Extracting lay paraphrases of specialized expressions from monolingual comparable medical corpora. In *Proceedings of the 2nd Workshop on Building and Using Comparable Corpora: from Parallel to Non-parallel Corpora*, Singapore.

Camille Dutrey, Houda Bouamor, Delphine Bernhard, and Aurélien Max. 2011. Local modifications and paraphrases in wikipedia's revision history. *SEPLN journal*, 46:51–58.

Cristina España Bonet, Marta Vila, M. Antònia Martí, and Horacio Rodríguez. 2009. Coco, a web interface for corpora compilation. *SEPLN journal*, 43.

Stanley Kok and Chris Brockett. 2010. Hitting the right paraphrases in good time. In *Proceedings of NAACL-HLT*, Los Angeles, USA.

Mirella Lapata and Frank Keller. 2005. Web-based Models for Natural Language Processing. *ACM Transactions on Speech and Language Processing*, 2(1):1–31.

Weigang Li, Ting Liu, Yu Zhang, Sheng Li, and Wei He. 2005. Automated generalization of phrasal paraphrases from the web. In *Proceedings of the IJCNLP Workshop on Paraphrasing*, Jeju Island, South Korea.

Nitin Madnani and Bonnie J. Dorr. 2010. Generating phrasal and sentential paraphrases: A survey of data-driven methods. *Computational Linguistics*, 36(3).

Nitin Madnani, Philip Resnik, Bonnie J. Dorr, and Richard Schwartz. 2008. Are multiple reference translations necessary? investigating the value of paraphrased reference translations in parameter optimization. In *Proceedings of AMTA*, Waikiki, USA.

Aurélien Max and Guillaume Wisniewski. 2010. Mining Naturally-occurring Corrections and Paraphrases from Wikipedia's Revision History. In *Proceedings of LREC 2010*, Valletta, Malta.

Aurélien Max and Michael Zock. 2008. Looking up phrase rephrasings via a pivot language. In *Proceedings of the COLING Workshop on Cognitive Aspects of the Lexicon*, Manchester, United Kingdom.

Aurélien Max. 2004. From controlled document authoring to interactive document normalization. In *Proceedings of COLING*, Geneva, Switzerland.

Diana McCarthy and Roberto Navigli. 2009. The english lexical substitution task. *Language Resources and Evaluation*, 43(2).

Andrew Mutton, Mark Dras, Stephen Wan, and Robert Dale. 2007. Gleu: Automatic evaluation of sentence-level fluency. In *Proceedings of ACL*, Prague, Czech Republic.

Andrew Mutton. 2006. *Evaluation of sentence grammaticality using Parsers and a Support Vector Machine*. Ph.D. thesis, Macquarie University.

Takashi Onishi, Masao Utiyama, and Eiichiro Sumita. 2010. Paraphrase Lattice for Statistical Machine Translation. In *Proceedings of ACL, Short Papers session*, Uppsala, Sweden.

Bo Pang, Kevin Knight, and Daniel Marcu. 2003. Syntax-based alignement of multiple translations: Extracting paraphrases and generating new sentences. In *Proceedings of NAACL-HLT*, Edmonton, Canada.

Slav Petrov and Dan Klein. 2007. Improved inference for unlexicalized parsing. In *Proceedings of NAACL-HLT*, Rochester, USA.

Chris Quirk, Chris Brockett, and William B. Dolan. 2004. Monolingual machine translation for paraphrase generation. In *Proceedings of EMNLP*, Barcelona, Spain.

Philip Resnik, Olivia Buzek, Chang Hu, Yakov Kronrod, Alex Quinn, and Benjamin B. Bederson. 2010. Improving translation via targeted paraphrasing. In *Proceedings of EMNLP*, Cambridge, MA.

Josh Schroeder, Trevor Cohn, and Philipp Koehn. 2009. Word lattices for multi-source translation. In *Proceedings of EACL*, Athens, Greece.

Matthew Snover, Nitin Madnani, Bonnie J. Dorr, and Richard Schwartz. 2010. TER-Plus: paraphrase, semantic, and alignment enhancements to Translation Edit Rate. *Machine Translation*, 23(2-3).

Kuansan Wang, Chris Thrasher, Evelyne Viegas, Xiaolong Li, and Bo-june (Paul) Hsu. 2010. An Overview of Microsoft Web N-gram Corpus and Applications. In *Proceedings of the NAACL-HLT Demonstration Session*, Los Angeles, USA.

Shiqi Zhao, Ting Liu, Xincheng Yuan, Sheng Li, and Yu Zhang. 2007. Automatic acquisition of context-specific lexical paraphrases. In *Proceedings of IJCAI 2007*, Hyderabad, India.

Shiqi Zhao, Xiang Lan, Ting Liu, and Sheng Li. 2009. Application-driven statistical paraphrase generation. In *Proceedings of the Joint ACL-IJCNLP*, Singapore.

Shiqi Zhao, Haifeng Wang, Ting Liu, , and Sheng Li. 2010. Leveraging multiple mt engines for paraphrase generation. In *Proceedings of COLING*, Beijing, China.

Zhemin Zhu, Delphine Bernhard, and Iryna Gurevych. 2010. A monolingual tree-based translation model for sentence simplification. In *Proceedings of COLING*, Beijing, China.

An Unsupervised Alignment Algorithm for Text Simplification Corpus Construction

Stefan Bott
TALN Research Group
Universitat Pompeu Fabra
C/Tanger 122 - Barcelona - 08018
Spain
stefan.bott@upf.edu

Horacio Saggion
TALN Research Group
Universitat Pompeu Fabra
C/Tanger 122 - Barcelona - 08018
Spain
horacio.saggion@upf.edu

Abstract

We present a method for the sentence-level alignment of short simplified text to the original text from which they were adapted. Our goal is to align a medium-sized corpus of parallel text, consisting of short news texts in Spanish with their simplified counterpart. No training data is available for this task, so we have to rely on unsupervised learning. In contrast to bilingual sentence alignment, in this task we can exploit the fact that the probability of sentence correspondence can be estimated from lexical similarity between sentences. We show that the algoithm employed performs better than a baseline which approaches the problem with a TF*IDF sentence similarity metric. The alignment algorithm is being used for the creation of a corpus for the study of text simplification in the Spanish language.

1 Introduction

Text simplification is the process of transforming a text into an equivalent which is more understandable for a target user. This simplification is beneficial for many groups of readers, such as language learners, elderly persons and people with other special reading and comprehension necessities. Simplified texts are characterized by a simple and direct style and a smaller vocabulary which substitutes infrequent and otherwise difficult words (such as long composite nouns, technical terms, neologisms and abstract concepts) by simpler corresponding expressions. Usually unnecessary details are omitted. Another characteristic trait of simplified texts is that usually only one main idea is expressed by a single sentence. This also means that in the simplification process complex sentences are often split into several smaller sentences.

The availability of a sentence-aligned corpus of original texts and their simplifications is of paramount importance for the study of simplification and for developing an automatic text simplification system. The different strategies that human editors employ to simplify texts are varied and have the effect that individual parts of the resulting text may either become shorter or longer than the original text. An editor may, for example, delete detailed information, making the text shorter. Or she may split complex sentences into various smaller sentences. As a result, simplified texts tend to be come shorter than the source, but often the number of sentences increases. Not all of the information presented in the original needs to be preserved but in general all of the information in the simplified text stems from the source text.

The need to align parallel texts arises from a larger need to create a medium size corpus which will allow the study of the editing process of simplifying text, as well as to serve as a gold standard to evaluate a text simplification system.

Sentence alignment for simplified texts is related to, but different from, the alignment of bilingual text and also from the alignment of summaries to an original text. Since the alignment of simplified sentences is a case of monolingual alignment the lexical similarity between two corresponding sentences can be taken as an indicator of correspondence.

This paper is organized as follows: Section 2 briefly introduces text simplification which contextualises this piece of research and Section 3 discusses some related work. In Section 4 we briefly describe the texts we are working with and in Section 5 we present the alignment algorithm. Section 6 presents the details of the experiment and its results. Finally, section 7 gives a concluding discussion and an outlook on future work.

2 Text Simplification

The simplification of written documents by humans has the objective of making texts more accessible to people with a linguistic handicap, however manual simplification of written documents is very expensive. If one considers people who cannot read documents with heavy information load or documents from authorities or governmental sources the percent of need for simplification is estimated at around 25% of the population, it is therefore of great importance to develop methods and tools to tackle this problem. Automatic text simplification, the task of transforming a given text into an "equivalent" which is less complex in vocabulary and form, aims at reducing the efforts and costs associated with human simplification. In addition to transforming texts into their simplification for human consumption, text simplification has other advantages since simpler texts can be processed more efficiently by different natural language processing processors such as parsers and used in applications such as machine translation, information extraction, question answering, and text summarization.

Early attempts to text simplification were based on rule-based methods where rules were designed following linguistic intuitions (Chandrasekar et al., 1996). Steps in the process included linguistic text analysis (including parsing) and pattern matching and transformation steps. Other computational models of text simplification included processes of analysis, transformation, and phrase re-generation (Siddharthan, 2002) also using rule-based techniques. In the PSET project (Carroll et al., 1998) the proposal is for a news simplification system for aphasic readers and particular attention is paid to linguistic phenomena such as passive constructions and coreference which are difficult to deal with by people with disabilities. The PorSimples project (Aluísio et al., 2008) has looked into simplification of the Portuguese language. The methodology consisted in the creation of a corpus of simplification at two different levels and on the use of the corpus to train a decision procedure for simplification based on linguistic features. Simplification decisions about whether to simplify a text or sentence have been studied following rule-based paradigms (Chandrasekar et al., 1996) or trainable systems (Petersen and Ostendorf, 2007) where a corpus of texts and their simplifications becomes necessary. Some resources are available for the English language such as parallel corpora created or studied in various projects (Barzilay and Elhadad, 2003; Feng et al., 2009; Petersen and Ostendorf, 2007; Quirk et al., 2004); however there is no parallel Spanish corpus available for research into text simplification. The algorithms to be presented here will be used to create such resource.

3 Related Work

The problem of sentence alignment was first tackled in the context of statistical machine translation. Gale and Church (1993) proposed a dynamic programming algorithm for the sentence-level alignment of translations that exploited two facts: the length of translated sentences roughly corresponds to the length of the original sentences and the sequence of sentences in translated text largely corresponds to the original order of sentences. With this simple approach they reached a high degree of accuracy.

Within the field of monolingual sentence alignment a large part of the work has concentrated on the alignment between text summaries and the source texts they summarize. Jing (2002) present an algorithm which aligns strings of words to pieces of text in an original document using a Hidden Markov Model. This approach is very specific to summary texts, concretely such summaries which have been produced by a "cut and paste" process. A work which is more closely related to our task is presented in Barzilay and Elhadad (2003). They carried out an experiment on two different versions of the *Encyclopedia Britannica* (the regular version and the *Britannica Elementary*) and aligned sentences in a four-step procedure: They clustered paragraphs into 'topic' groups, then they trained a binary classifier (aligned or not aligned) for paragraph pairs on a handcrafted set of sentence alignments. After that they grouped all paragraphs of unseen text pairs into the same topic clusters as in the first step and aligned the texts on the paragraph level, allowing for multiple matches. Finally they aligned the sentences within the already aligned paragraphs. Their similarity measure, both for paragraphs and sentences, was based on cosine distance of word overlap. Nelken and Shieber (2006) improve over Barzilay and Elhadad's work: They use the same data set, but they base their similarity measure for aligning sentences on a TF*IDF score. Although this score can be obtained without any training, they apply logistic regression on these scores and train two parameters of this regression model on the training data. Both of these approaches can be tuned by parameter settings, which results in a trade-off between precision and recall. Barzilay and Elhadad report a precision of 76.9% when the recall reaches 55.8%. Nelken and Shieber raise this value to 83.1% with the same recall level and show that TF*IDF is a much better sentence similarity measure. Zhu et al. (2010) even report a precision of 91.3% (at the same fixed recall value of 55.8%) for the alignment of simple English Wikipedia articles to the English Wikipedia counterparts using Nelken and Shieber's TF*IDF score, but their alignment was part of a larger problem setting and they do not discuss further details.

We consider that our task is not directly comparable to this previous work: the texts we are working with are direct simplifications of the source texts. So we can assume that all information in the simplified text must stem from the original text. In addition we can make the simplifying assumption that there are one-to-many, but no many-to-one relations between source sentences and simplified sentences, a simplification which largely holds for our corpus. This means that all target sentences must find at least one alignment to a source sentence, but not vice versa. Nelken and Shieber make the interesting observation that dynamic programming, as used by Gale and Church (1991) fails to work in the monolingual case. Their test data consisted of pairs of encyclopedia articles which presented a large intersection of factual information, but which was not necessarily presented in the same order. The corpus we are working with, however, largely preserves the order in which information is presented.

4 Dataset

We are working with a corpus of 200 news articles in Spanish covering the following topics: National News, Society, International News and Culture. Each of the texts is being adapted by the DILES Research Group from Universidad Autónoma de Madrid (Anula, 2007). Original and adapted examples of texts in Spanish can be seen in Figure 1 (the texts are adaptations carried out by DILES for Revista "La Plaza"). The texts are being processed using part-of-speech tagging, named entity recognition, and parsing in order to create an automatically annotated corpus. The bi-texts are first aligned using the tools to be described in this paper and then post-edited with the help of a bi-text editor provided in the GATE framework (Cunningham et al., 2002). Figure 2 shows the texts in the alignment editor. This tool is however insufficient for our purposes since it does not provide mechanisms for uploading the alignments produced outside the GATE framework and for producing stand-alone versions of the bi-texts; we have therefore extended the functionalities of the tool for the purpose of corpus creation.

5 Algorithm

Our algorithm is based on two intuitions about simplified texts (as found in our corpus): As repeatedly observed sentences in simplified texts use similar words to those in the original sentences that they stem from (even if some of the words may have undergone lexical simplification). The second observation is very specific to our data: the order in which information is presented in simplified texts roughly corresponds to the order of the information in the source text. So sentences which are close to each other in simplified texts correspond to original sentences which are also close to each other in the source text. In many cases, two adjacent simplified sentences even correspond to one single sentence in the source text. This leads us to apply a simple Hidden Markov Model which allows for a sequential classification.

Firstly, we define an alignment as a pair of sentences as

$$\langle source\_sent_i, target\_sent_j \rangle,$$

Original Text	Adapted Text
Un Plan Global desde tu hogar El Programa GAP (Global Action Plan) es una iniciativa que se desarrolla en distintos países y que pretende disminuir las emisiones de CO2, principales causantes del cambio climático y avanzar hacia hábitos más sostenibles en aspectos como el consumo de agua y energía, la movilidad o la gestión de los residuos domésticos. San Sebastián de los Reyes se ha adherido a este Programa. Toda la información disponible para actuar desde el hogar en la construcción de un mundo más sostenible se puede encontrar en ssreyes.org o programagap.es.	Un Plan Global desde tu hogar San Sebastián de los Reyes se ha unido al Plan de Acción Global (GAP). El Plan es una iniciativa para luchar contra el cambio climático desde tu casa. Los objetivos del Plan son: Disminuir nuestros gastos domésticos de agua y energía. Reducir los efectos dañinos que producimos en el planeta con nuestros residuos. Mejorar la calidad de vida de nuestra ciudad. Tienes más información en ssreyes.org y en programagap.es. Apúntate al programa GAP y descárgate los manuales con las propuestas para conservar el planeta.

Figure 1: Original Full Document and Easy-to-Read Version

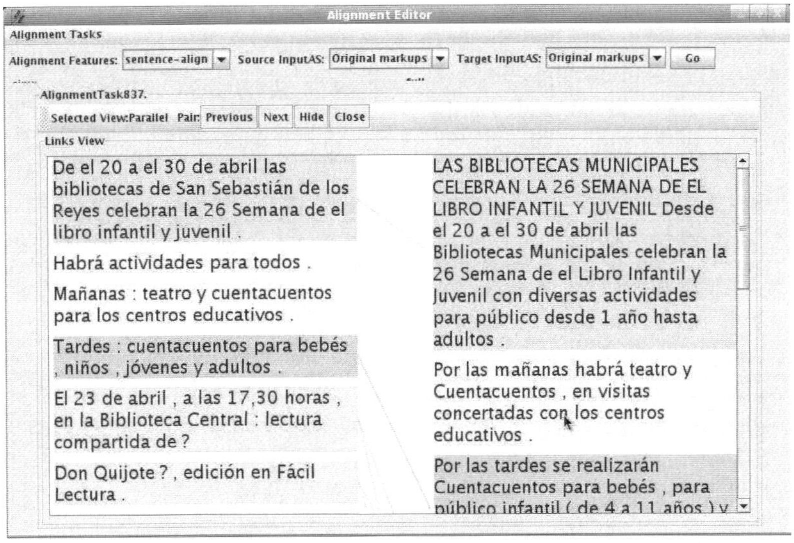

Figure 2: The Alignment Editor with Text and Adaptation

where a target sentence belongs to the simplified text and the source sentence belongs to the original sentence. Applying standard Bayesian decomposition, the probability of an alignment to a given target text can be calculated as follows:

$$P(align_1^n|target\_sent_1^m) = \frac{P(align_1^n)P(target\_sent_1^m|align_1^n)}{P(target\_sent_1^m)}$$

Since $P(target\_sent_1^m)$ is constant we can calculate the most probable alignment sequence $\widehat{align}$ as follows:

$$\widehat{align} = arg\ max P(align_1^n)\ P(target\_sent_1^m|align_1^n) = arg\ max \prod_{i=1}^{n} P(align_{i,j})P(target\_sent_j|align_{i,j})$$

This leaves us with two measures: a measure of sentence similarity (the probability of alignment proper) and a measure of consistency, under the assumption that a consistent simplified text presents the information in the same order as it is presented in the source text. In order to determine $\widehat{align}$, we apply the *Viterbi* algorithm (Viterbi, 1967).

Sentence similarity can be calculated as follows:

$$P(word_1^l|target\_sent_j) = \prod_{k=1}^{l} \frac{P(target\_sent_j|word_k)P(target\_sent_j)}{P(word_k)}$$

where $word_1^l$ is the sequence of words in the source sentence i and l is the length of sentence i.

This similarity measure is different from both word overlap cosine distance and TF*IDF. It is, however, similar to TF*IDF in that it penalizes words which are frequent in the source text and boosts the score for less frequent words. In addition we eliminated a short list of stopwords from the calculation, but this has no significant effect on the general performance.

Note that $P(word_k)$ may correspond to a MLE of 0 since simplified texts often use different (and simpler) words and add connectors, conjunctions and the like. For this reason we have to recalculate $P(word_k)$ according to a distortion probability α. Distortion is taken here as the process of word insertion or lexical changes. α is a small constant, which could be determined empirically, but since no training data is available we estimated α for our experiment and set it by hand to a value of 0.0075. Even if we had to estimate α we found that the performance of the system is robust regarding its value: even for unrealistic values like 0.0001 and 0.1 the performance only drops by two percent points.

$$P(word_k|distortion) = \\ (1-\alpha)P(word_k) + \alpha(1 - P(word_k))$$

For the consistency measure we made the Markov assumption that each alignment $align_{i,j}$ only depends on the proceeding alignment $align_{i-1,j'}$. We assume that this is the probability of a distance *d* between the corresponding sentences of $source\_sent_{i-1}$ and $source\_sent_i$, i.e. $P(source\_sent_i|align_{i-1,j-k})$ for each possible jump distance k. Since long jumps are relatively rare, we used a normalized even probability distribution for all jump lengths greater than 2 and smaller than -1.

Since we have no training data, we have to initially set these probabilities by hand. We do this by assuming that all jump distances *k* in the range between -1 and 2 are distributed evenly and larger jump distances have an accumulated probability mass corresponding to one of the local jump distances. Although this model for sentence transitions is apparently oversimplistic and gives a very bad estimate for each $P(source\_sent_i|align_{i-1,j-k})$, the probabilities for $P(align_1^n)$ give a counterweight to these bad estimates. What we can expect is, that after running the aligner once, using very unreliable transitions probability estimates, the output of the aligner is a set of alignments with an implicit alignment sequence. Taking this alignment sequence, we can calculate new maximum likelihood estimates for each jump distance $P(source\_sent_i|align_{i-1,j-k})$ again, and we can expect that these new estimates are much better than the original ones.

For this reason we apply the Viterbi classifier iteratively: The first iteration employs the hand set values. Then we run the classifier and determine the values for $P(source\_sent_i|align_{i-1,j-k})$ on its output. Then we run the classifier again, with the new model and so on. Interestingly values for $P(source\_sent_i|align_{i-1,j-k})$ emerge after as little as two iterations. After the first iteration, precision already lies only 1.2 percent points and recall 1.3 points below the stable values. We will comment on this finding in Section 7.

6 Experiment and Results

Our goal is to align a larger corpus of Spanish short news texts with their simplified counterparts. At the moment, however, we only have a small sample of this corpus available. The size of this corpus sample is 1840 words of simplified text (145 sentences) which correspond to 2456 (110 sentences) of source text. We manually created a gold standard which includes all the correct alignments between simplified and source sentences. The results of the classifier were calculated against this gold standard.

As a baseline we used a TF*IDF score based method which chooses for each sentence in the simplified text the sentence with the minimal word vector distance. The procedure is as follows: each sentence in the original and simplified document is represented in the vector space model using a term vector (Saggion, 2008). Each term (e.g. token) is weithed using as TF the frequency of the term in the document and IDF = $log(N+1/M_t+1)$ where M_t is the number of sentences [1] containing t and N is the number of sentences in the corpus (counts are obtained from the set of documents to align). As similarity metric between vectors we use the cosine of the angle between the two vectors given in the following formula:

[1]The relevant unit for the calculation of IDF (the D in IDF) here is the sentence, not the document as in information retrieval.

$$\text{cosine}(s_1, s_2) = \frac{\sum_{i=1}^{n} w_{i,s_1} * w_{i,s_2}}{\sqrt{\sum_{i=1}^{n}(w_{i,s_1})^2} * \sqrt{\sum_{i=1}^{n}(w_{i,s_2})^2}}$$

Here s_1 and s_2 are the sentence vectors and w_{i,s_k} is the weight of term i in sentence s_k. We align all simplified sentences (i.e. for the time being no cut-off has been used to identify new material in the simplified text).

For the calculation of the first baseline we calculate IDF over the sentences in whole corpus. Nelken and Shieber (2006) argue that that the relevant unit for this calculation should be each document for the following reason: Some words are much more frequent in some texts than they are in others. For example the word *unicorn* is relatively infrequent in English and it it may also be infrequent in a given colletion of texts. So this word is highly discriminative and it's IDF will be relatively high. In a specific text about imagenary creatures, however, the same word *unicorn* may be much more frequent and hence it's discrimiative power is much lower. For this reason we calcuated a second baseline, where we calculate the IDF only on the sentences of the relevanct texts.

Results of aligning all sentences in our sample corpus using both the baseline and the HMM algorithms are given in Table 6.

	precision	recall
HMM aligner	82.4%	80.9%
alignment only	81.13%	79.63%
TF*IDF + transitions	76.1%	73.5%
TF*IDF (document)	75.47%	74.07%
TF*IDF (full corpus)	62.2%	61.1%

If we compare these results to those presented by Nelken and Shieber (2006), we can observe that we obtain a comparable precision, but the recall improves dramatically from 55.8% (with their specific feature setting) to 82.4%. Our TF*IDF baselines are not directly comparable comparable to Nelken and Shieber's results. The reason why we cannot compare our results directly is that Nelken and Shieber use supervised learning in order to optimize the transformation of TF*IDF scores into probabilities and we had no training data available.

We included the additional scores for our system, when no transition probabilities are included in the calculation of the optimal alignment sequence and the score comes only from the probabilies of our clalculation of lexical similarity between sentences (*alignment only*). These scores show that a large part of the good performance comes from lexical similarity and sequencial classification only give an additional final boost, a fact which was already observed by Nelken and Shieber. We also attribute the fact that the system alrives at stable values after two iterations to the same efect: lexical similarity seems to have a much bigger effect on the general performance. Still our probability-based similarity meassure clearly outperforms the TF*IDF baselines.

7 Discussion and Outlook

We have argued above that our task is not directly comparable to Nelken and Shieber's alignment of two versions of Encyclopedia articles. First of all, the texts we are working with are simplified texts in a much stricter sense: they are the result of an editing process which turns a source text into a simplified version. This allows us to use sequential classification which is usually not successful for monolingual sentence alignment. This helps especially in the case of simplified sentences which have been largely re-written with simpler vocabulary. These cases would normally be hard to align correctly. Although it could be argued that the characteristics of such genuinely simplified text makes the alignment task somewhat easier, we would like to stress that the alignment method we present makes no use of any kind of training data, in contrast to Barzilay and Elhadad (2003) and, to a minor extent, Nelken and Shieber (2006).

Although we started out from a very specific need to align a corpus with reliably simplified news articles, we are confident that our approach can be applied in other circumstances. For future work we are planning to apply this algorithm in combination of a version of Barzilay and Elhadad's macro-alignment and use sequential classification only for the alignment of sentences within already aligned paragraphs. This would make our work directly comparable. We are also planning to test our algorithm, especially the sentence similarity measure it uses, on data which is similar the data Barzilay and Elhadad (and also Nelken and Shieber) used in their experiment.

Finally, the alignment tool will be used to sentence-align a medium-sized parallel Spanish corpus of news and their adaptations that will be a much needed resource for the study of text simplification and other natural language processing applications. Since the size of the corpus we have available at the moment is relatively modest, we are also investigating alternative resources which could allow us to create a larger parallel corpus.

Acknowledgments

We thank three anonymous reviewers for their comments and suggestions which help improve the final version of this paper. The research described in this paper arises from a Spanish research project called Simplext: An automatic system for text simplification (`http://www.simplext.es`). Simplext is led by Technosite and partially funded by the Ministry of Industry, Tourism and Trade of the Government of Spain, by means of the National Plan of Scientific Research, Development and Technological Innovation (I+D+i), within strategic Action of Telecommunications and Information Society (Avanza Competitiveness, with file number TSI-020302-2010-84). We thanks the Department of Information and Communication Technologies at UPF for their support. We are grateful to Programa Ramón y Cajal from Ministerio de Ciencia e Innovación, Spain.

References

Sandra M. Aluísio, Lucia Specia, Thiago Alexandre Salgueiro Pardo, Erick Galani Maziero, and Renata Pontin de Mattos Fortes. 2008. Towards brazilian portuguese automatic text simplification systems. In *ACM Symposium on Document Engineering*, pages 240–248.

A. Anula. 2007. Tipos de textos, complejidad lingüística y facilicitación lectora. In *Actas del Sexto Congreso de Hispanistas de Asia*, pages 45–61.

Regina Barzilay and Noemi Elhadad. 2003. Sentence alignment for monolingual comparable corpora. In *In Proceedings of the 2003 conference on Empirical methods in natural language processing*, pages 25–32.

John Carroll, Guido Minnen, Yvonne Canning, Siobhan Devlin, and John Tait. 1998. Practical simplification of english newspaper text to assist aphasic readers. In *In Proc. of AAAI-98 Workshop on Integrating Artificial Intelligence and Assistive Technology*, pages 7–10.

Raman Chandrasekar, Christine Doran, and Bangalore Srinivas. 1996. Motivations and methods for text simplification. In *COLING*, pages 1041–1044.

H. Cunningham, D. Maynard, K. Bontcheva, and V. Tablan. 2002. GATE: A framework and graphical development environment for robust NLP tools and applications. In *Proceedings of the 40th Anniversary Meeting of the Association for Computational Linguistics*.

Lijun Feng, Noemie Elhadad, and Matt Huenerfauth. 2009. Cognitively motivated features for readability assessment. In *EACL*, pages 229–237.

William A. Gale and Kenneth W. Church. 1993. A program for aligning sentences in bilingual corpora. *Computational Linguistics*.

Hongyan Jing. 2002. Using hidden markov modeling to decompose human-written summaries. *Comput. Linguist.*, 28:527–543, December.

Rani Nelken and Stuart M. Shieber. 2006. Towards robust context-sensitive sentence alignment for monolingual corpora. In *In 11th Conference of the European Chapter of the Association for Computational Linguistics*.

Sarah E. Petersen and Mari Ostendorf. 2007. Text simplification for language learners: a corpus analysis. In *In Proc. of Workshop on Speech and Language Technology for Education*.

Chris Quirk, Chris Brockett, and William Dolan. 2004. Monolingual machine translation for paraphrase generation. In *In Proceedings of the 2004 Conference on Empirical Methods in Natural Language Processing*, pages 142–149.

H. Saggion. 2008. SUMMA: A Robust and Adaptable Summarization Tool. *Traitement Automatique des Langues*, 49(2):103–125.

Advaith Siddharthan. 2002. An architecture for a text simplification system. In *In LEC 02: Proceedings of the Language Engineering Conference (LEC02*, pages 64–71.

A. Viterbi. 1967. Error bounds for convolutional codes and an asymptotically optimum decoding algorithm. *IEEE Transactions on Information Theory*, 13:260–269.

Zhemin Zhu, Delphine Bernhard, and Iryna Gurevych. 2010. A monolingual tree-based translation model for sentence simplification. In *Proceedings of The 23rd International Conference on Computational Linguistics*, pages 1353–1361, Beijing, China, Aug.

Comparing Phrase-based and Syntax-based Paraphrase Generation

Sander Wubben
Tilburg University
P.O. Box 90135
5000 LE Tilburg
The Netherlands
s.wubben@uvt.nl

Erwin Marsi
NTNU
Sem Saelandsvei 7-9
NO-7491 Trondheim
Norway
emarsi@idi.ntnu.no

Antal van den Bosch
Tilburg University
P.O. Box 90135
5000 LE Tilburg
The Netherlands
antal.vdnbosch@uvt.nl

Emiel Krahmer
Tilburg University
P.O. Box 90135
5000 LE Tilburg
The Netherlands
e.j.krahmer@uvt.nl

Abstract

Paraphrase generation can be regarded as machine translation where source and target language are the same. We use the Moses statistical machine translation toolkit for paraphrasing, comparing phrase-based to syntax-based approaches. Data is derived from a recently released, large scale (2.1M tokens) paraphrase corpus for Dutch. Preliminary results indicate that the phrase-based approach performs better in terms of NIST scores and produces paraphrases at a greater distance from the source.

1 Introduction

One of the challenging properties of natural language is that the same semantic content can typically be expressed by many different surface forms. As the ability to deal with paraphrases holds great potential for improving the coverage of NLP systems, a substantial body of research addressing recognition, extraction and generation of paraphrases has emerged (Androutsopoulos and Malakasiotis, 2010; Madnani and Dorr, 2010). Paraphrase Generation can be regarded as a translation task in which source and target language are the same. Both Paraphrase Generation and Machine Translation (MT) are instances of Text-To-Text Generation, which involves transforming one text into another, obeying certain restrictions. Here these restrictions are that the generated text must be grammatically well-formed and semantically/translationally equivalent to the source text. Addionally Paraphrase Generation requires that the output should differ from the input to a certain degree.

The similarity between Paraphrase Generation and MT suggests that methods and tools originally developed for MT could be exploited for Paraphrase Generation. One popular approach – arguably the most successful so far – is Statistical Phrase-based Machine Translation (PBMT), which learns phrase translation rules from aligned bilingual text corpora (Och et al., 1999; Vogel et al., 2000; Zens et al., 2002; Koehn et al., 2003). Prior work has explored the use of PBMT for paraphrase generation (Quirk et al., 2004; Bannard and Callison-Burch, 2005; Madnani et al., 2007; Callison-Burch, 2008; Zhao et al., 2009; Wubben et al., 2010)

However, since many researchers believe that PBMT has reached a performance ceiling, ongoing research looks into more structural approaches to statistical MT (Marcu and Wong, 2002; Och and Ney, 2004; Khalilov and Fonollosa, 2009). Syntax-based MT attempts to extract translation rules in terms of syntactic constituents or subtrees rather than arbitrary phrases, presupposing syntactic structures for source, target or both languages. Syntactic information might lead to better results in the area of grammatical well-formedness, and unlike phrase-based MT that uses contiguous n-grams, syntax enables the modeling of long-distance translation patterns.

While the verdict on whether or not this approach leads to any significant performance gain is still out, a similar line of reasoning would suggest that syntax-based paraphrasing may offer similar advantages over phrase-based paraphrasing. Considering the fact that the success of PBMT can partly be attributed to the abundance of large parallel corpora, and that sufficiently large parallel corpora are still lacking for paraphrase generation, using more linguistically motivated methods might prove beneficial for paraphrase generation. At the same time, automatic syntactic analysis introduces errors in the parse trees, as no syntactic parser is perfect. Likewise, automatic alignment of syntactic phrases may be prone to errors.

The main contribution of this paper is a systematic comparison between phrase-based and syntax-based paraphrase generation using an off-the-shelf statistical machine translation (SMT) decoder, namely Moses (Koehn et al., 2007) and the word-alignment tool GIZA++ (Och and Ney, 2003). Training data derives from a new, large scale (2.1M tokens) paraphrase corpus for Dutch, which has been recently released.

The paper is organized as follows. Section 2 reviews the paraphrase corpus from which provides training and test data. Next, Section 3 describes the paraphrase generation methods and the experimental setup. Results are presented in Section 4. In Section 5 we discuss our findings and formulate our conclusions.

2 Corpus

The main bottleneck in building SMT systems is the need for a substantial amount of parallel aligned text. Likewise, exploiting SMT for paraphrasing requires large amounts of monolingual parallel text. However, paraphrase corpora are scarce; the situation is more dire than in MT, and this has caused some studies to focus on the automatic harvesting of paraphrase corpora. The use of monolingual parallel text corpora was first suggested by Barzilay and McKeown (2001), who built their corpus using various alternative human-produced translations of literary texts and then applied machine learning or multi-sequence alignment for extracting paraphrases. In a similar vein, Pang et al. (2003) used a corpus of alternative English translations of Chinese news stories in combination with a syntax-based algorithm that automatically builds word lattices, in which paraphrases can be identified.

So-called *comparable* monolingual corpora, for instance independently written news reports describing the same event, in which some pairs of sentences exhibit partial semantic overlap have also been investigated (Shinyama et al., 2002; Barzilay and Lee, 2003; Shen et al., 2006; Wubben et al., 2009)

The first manually collected paraphrase corpus is the Microsoft Research Paraphrase (MSRP) Corpus (Dolan et al., 2004), consisting of 5,801 sentence pairs, sampled from a larger corpus of news articles. However, it is rather small and contains no subsentential allignments. Cohn et al. (2008) developed a parallel monolingual corpus of 900 sentence pairs annotated at the word and phrase level. However, all of these corpora are small from an SMT perspective.

Recently a new large-scale paraphrase corpus for Dutch, the DAESO corpus, was released. The corpus contains both samples of parallel and comparable text in which similar sentences, phrases and words are aligned. One part of the corpus is manually aligned, whereas another part is automatically aligned using a data-driven aligner trained on the first part. The DAESO corpus is extensively described in (Marsi and Krahmer, 2011); the summary here is limited to aspects relevant to the work at hand.

The corpus contains the following types of text: (1) alternative translations in Dutch of three literary works of fiction; (2) autocue text from televion broadcast news as read by the news reader, and the corresponding subtitles; (3) headlines from similar news articles obtained from Google News Dutch; (4) press releases about the same news topic from two different press agencies; (5) similar answers retrieved from a document collection in the medical domain, originally created for evaluating question-answering systems.

In a first step, similar sentences were automatically aligned, after which alignments were manually corrected. In the case of the parallel book texts, aligned sentences are (approximate) paraphrases. To a lesser degree, this is also true for the news headlines. The autocue-subtitle pairs are mostly examples of sentence compression, as the subtitle tends to be a compressed version of the read autocue text. In contrast, the press releases and the QA answers, are characterized by a great deal of one-to-many sentence alignments, as well as sentences left unaligned, as is to be expected in comparable text. Most sentences in these types of text tend to have only partial overlap in meaning.

Table 1: Properties of the manually aligned corpus

	Autosub	Books	Headlines	News	QA	Overall
aligned trees	18 338	6 362	32 627	11 052	118	68 497
tokens	217 959	115 893	179 629	162 361	2 230	678 072
tokens/sent	11.89	18.22	5.51	14.69	18.90	9.90
nodes	365 157	191 636	318 399	271 192	3734	1 150 118
nodes/tree	19.91	30.12	9.76	24.54	31.64	16.79
uniquely aligned trees (%)	92.93	92.49	84.57	63.61	50.00	84.10
aligned nodes (%)	73.53	66.83	73.58	53.62	38.62	67.62

Next, aligned sentences were tokenized and parsed with the Alpino parser for Dutch (Bouma et al., 2001). The parser provides a relatively theory-neutral syntactic analysis which is a blend of phrase structure analysis and dependency analysis, with a backbone of phrasal constituents and arcs labeled with syntactic function/dependency labels.

The alignments not only concern paraphrases in the strict sense, i.e., expressions that are semantically equivalent, but extend to expressions that are semantically similar in less strict ways, for instance, where one phrase is either more specific or more general than the related phrase. For this reason, alignments are also labeled according to a limited set of semantic similarity relations. Since these relations were not used in the current study, we will not discuss them further here.

The corpus comprises over 2.1 million tokens, 678 thousand of which are manually annotated and 1,511 thousand are automatically processed.

To give a more complete overview of the sizes of different corpus segments, some properties of the manually aligned corpus are listed in Table 1. Properties of the automatically aligned part are similar, except for the fact that it only contains text of the news and QA type.

3 Paraphrase generation

Phrase-based MT models consider translation as a mapping of small text chunks, with possible re-ordering (Och and Ney, 2004). Operations such as insertion, deletion and many-to-one, one-to-many or many-to-many translation are all covered in the structure of the phrase table. Phrase-based models have been used most prominently in the past decade, as they have shown to outperform other approaches (Callison-Burch et al., 2009).

One issue with the phrase-based approach is that recursion is not handled explicitly. It is generally acknowledged that language contains recursive structures up to certain depths. So-called hierarchical models have introduced the inclusion of non-terminals in the mapping rules, to allow for recursion (Chiang et al., 2005). However, using a generic non-terminal X can introduce many substitutions in translations that do not make sense. By making the non-terminals explicit, using syntactic categories such as NPs and VPs, this phenomenon is constrained, resulting in *syntax-based* translation. Instead of phrase translations, translation rules in terms of syntactic constituents or subtrees are extracted, presupposing the availability of syntactic structures for source, target, or both languages.

Incorporating syntax can guide the translation process and unlike phrase-based MT syntax it enables the modeling of long-distance translation patterns. Syntax-based systems may parse the data on the target side (string-to-tree), source side (tree-to-string), or both (tree-to-tree).

In our experiments we use tree-to-tree syntax-based MT. We also experiment with relaxing the parses by a method proposed under the label of syntax-augmented machine translation (SAMT), described in (Zollmann and Venugopal, 2006). This method combines any neighboring nodes and labels previously unlabeled nodes, removing the syntactic constraint on the grammar[1].

We train all systems on the DAESO data (218,102 lines of aligned sentences) and test on a held-out set consisting of manually aligned headlines that ap-

[1]This method is implemented in the Moses package in the program relax-parse as option SAMT 4

Table 2: Examples of output of the phrase-based and syntax-based systems

Source	jongen (7) zwaargewond na aanrijding	*boy (7) severely-injured after crash*
Phrase-based	7-jarige gewond na botsing	*7-year-old injured after collision*
Syntax-based	jongen (7) zwaar gewond na aanrijding	*boy (7) severely injured after crash*
Source	jeugdwerkloosheid daalt vooral bij voldoende opleiding	*youth-unemployment drops especially with adequate training*
Phrase-based	werkloosheid jongeren daalt , vooral bij voldoende studie	*unemployment youths drops, especially with sufficient study*
Syntax-based	* jeugdwerkloosheid daalt vooral in voldoende opleiding	*youth-unemployment drops especially in adequate training*
Source	kritiek op boetebeleid ns	*criticism of fining-policy ns*
Phrase-based	* kritiek op de omstreden boetebeleid en	*criticism of the controversial and*
Syntax-based	kritiek op omstreden boetebeleid nederlandse spoorwegen	*criticism of controversial fining-policy dutch railways*
Source	weer bestuurders radboud weg	*again directors radboud [hospital] leaving*
Phrase-based	* weer de weg ziekenhuis	*again the leaving hospital*
Syntax-based	alweer bestuurders ziekenhuis weg	*yet-again directors hospital leaving*

peared in May 2006.[2] We test on 773 headlines that have three or more aligned paraphrasing reference headlines. We use an SRILM (Stolcke, 2002) language model trained on the Twente news corpus[3].

To investigate the effect of the amount of training data on results, we also train a phrase-based model on more data by adding more aligned headlines originating from data crawled in 2010 and aligned using $tf.idf$ scores over headline clusters and Cosine similarity as described in (Wubben et al., 2009), resulting in an extra 612,158 aligned headlines.

Evaluation is based on the assumption that a good paraphrase is well-formed and semantically similar but structurally different from the source sentence. We therefore score the generated paraphrases not only by an MT metric (we use NIST scores), but also factor in the edit distance between the input sentence and the output sentence. We take the 10-best generated paraphrases and select from these the one most dissimilar from the source sentence in term of Levenshtein distance on tokens. We then weigh NIST scores according to their corresponding sentence Levenshtein Distance, to calculate a weighted average score. This implies that we penalize systems that provide output at Levenshtein distance 0, which are essentially copies of the input, and not paraphrases. Formally, the score is computed as follows:

$$NIST_{weighted_{LD}} = \alpha \frac{\sum_{i=LD(1..8)} (i * N_i * NIST_i)}{\sum_{i=LD(1..8)} (i * N_i)}$$

where α is the percentage of output phrases that have a sentence Levenshtein Distance higher than 0. Instead of NIST scores, other MT evaluation scores can be plugged into this formula, such as METEOR (Lavie and Agarwal, 2007) for languages for which paraphrase data is available.

4 Results

Figure 1 shows NIST scores per Levenshtein Distance. It can be observed that overall the NIST score decreases as the distance to the input increases, indicating that more distant paraphrases are of less quality. The relaxed syntax-based approach (SAMT) performs mildly better than the standard syntax-based approach, but performs worse than the phrase-based approach. The distribution of generated paraphrases per Levenshtein Distance is shown in Figure 2. It reveals that the Syntax-based approaches tend to stay closer to the source than the phrase-based approaches.

In Table 2 a few examples of output from both Phrase- and Syntax-based systems are given. The

[2]Syntactic trees were converted to the XML format used by Moses for syntax-based MT. A minor complication is that the word order in the tree is different from the word order in the corresponding sentence in about half of the cases. The technical reason is that Alpino internally produces dependency structures that can be non-projective. Conversion to a phrase structure tree therefore necessitates moving some words to a different position in the tree. We performed a subsequent reordering of the trees, moving terminals to make the word order match the surface word order.

[3]`http://www.vf.utwente.nl/~druid/TwNC/TwNC-main.html`

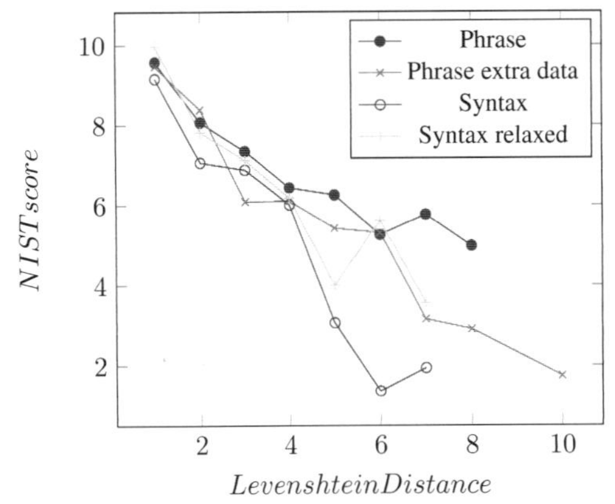

Figure 1: NIST scores per Levenshtein distance

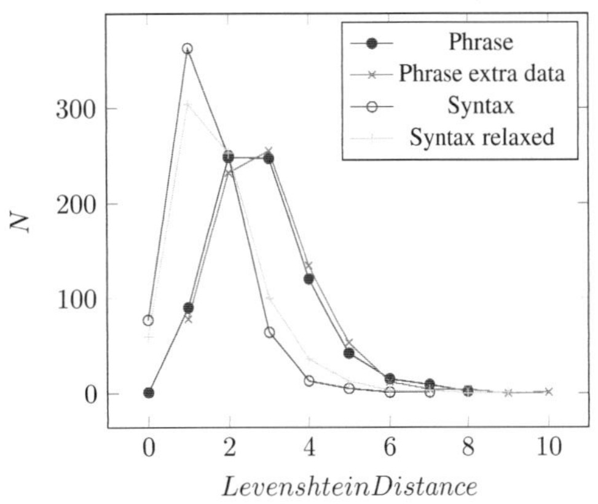

Figure 2: Distribution of generated paraphrases per Levenshtein distance

top two examples show sentences where the phrase-based approach scores better, and the bottom two show examples where the syntax-based approach scores better. In general, we observe that the phrase-based approach is often more drastic with its changes, as shown also in Figure 2. The syntax-based approach is less risky, and reverts more to single-word substitution.

The weighted NIST score for the phrase-based approach is 7.14 versus 6.75 for the syntax-based approach. Adding extra data does not improve the phrase-based approach, as it yields a score of 6.47, but the relaxed method does improve the syntax-based approach (7.04).

5 Discussion and conclusion

We have compared a phrase-based MT approach to paraphrasing with a syntax-based MT approach. The Phrase-based approach performs better in terms of NIST score weighted by edit distance of the output. In general, the phrase-based MT system performs more edits and these edits seem to be more reliable than the edits done by the Syntax-based approach. A relaxed Syntax-based approach performs better, while adding more data to the Phrase-based approach does not yield better results. To gain a better understanding of the quality of the output generated by the different approaches, it would be desirable to present the output of the different systems to human judges. In future work, we intend to compare the effects of using manual word alignments from the DAESO corpus instead of the automatic alignments produced by GIZA++. We also wish to further explore the effect of the nature of the data that we train on: the DAESO corpus consists of various data sources from different domains. Our aim is also to incorporate the notion of dissimilarity into the paraphrase model, by adding dissimilarity scores to the model.

References

Ion Androutsopoulos and Prodromos Malakasiotis. 2010. A survey of paraphrasing and textual entailment methods. *Journal of Artificial Intelligence Research*, 38:135–187, May.

Colin Bannard and Chris Callison-Burch. 2005. Paraphrasing with bilingual parallel corpora. In *ACL '05: Proceedings of the 43rd Annual Meeting on Association for Computational Linguistics*, pages 597–604, Morristown, NJ, USA. Association for Computational Linguistics.

Regina Barzilay and Lillian Lee. 2003. Learning to paraphrase: an unsupervised approach using multiple-sequence alignment. In *NAACL '03: Proceedings of the 2003 Conference of the North American Chapter of the Association for Computational Linguistics on Human Language Technology*, pages 16–23, Morristown, NJ, USA. Association for Computational Linguistics.

Regina Barzilay and Kathleen McKeown. 2001. Extracting paraphrases from a parallel corpus. In *Proceedings of Meeting of the Association for Computational Linguistics*, pages 50–57, Toulouse, France.

Gosse Bouma, Gertjan van Noord, and Robert Malouf. 2001. Alpino: Wide-coverage computational analysis of Dutch. In Walter Daelemans, Khalil Sima'an, Jorn Veenstra, and Jakub Zavre, editors, *Computational Linguistics in the Netherlands 2000.*, pages 45–59. Rodopi, Amsterdam, New York.

Chris Callison-Burch, Philipp Koehn, Christof Monz, and Josh Schroeder. 2009. Findings of the 2009 Workshop on Statistical Machine Translation. In *Proceedings of the Fourth Workshop on Statistical Machine Translation*, pages 1–28, Athens, Greece, March. Association for Computational Linguistics.

Chris Callison-Burch. 2008. Syntactic constraints on paraphrases extracted from parallel corpora. In *Proceedings of the Conference on Empirical Methods in Natural Language Processing*, EMNLP '08, pages 196–205, Stroudsburg, PA, USA. Association for Computational Linguistics.

David Chiang, Adam Lopez, Nitin Madnani, Christof Monz, Philip Resnik, and Michael Subotin. 2005. The hiero machine translation system: extensions, evaluation, and analysis. In *Proceedings of the conference on Human Language Technology and Empirical Methods in Natural Language Processing*, HLT '05, pages 779–786, Stroudsburg, PA, USA. Association for Computational Linguistics.

Trevor Cohn, Chris Callison-Burch, and Mirella Lapata. 2008. Constructing corpora for the development and evaluation of paraphrase systems. *Computational Linguistics*, 34(4):597–614.

Bill Dolan, Chris Quirk, and Chris Brockett. 2004. Unsupervised construction of large paraphrase corpora: Exploiting massively parallel news sources. In *Proceedings of the 20th International Conference on Computational Linguistics*, pages 350–356, Morristown, NJ, USA.

Maxim Khalilov and José A. R. Fonollosa. 2009. N-gram-based statistical machine translation versus syntax augmented machine translation: comparison and system combination. In *Proceedings of the 12th Conference of the European Chapter of the Association for Computational Linguistics*, EACL '09, pages 424–432, Stroudsburg, PA, USA. Association for Computational Linguistics.

Philip Koehn, Franz Josef Och, and Daniel Marcu. 2003. Statistical phrase-based translation. In *Proceedings of the 2003 Conference of the North American Chapter of the Association for Computational Linguistics on Human Language Technology-Volume 1*, pages 48–54. Association for Computational Linguistics.

Philipp Koehn, Hieu Hoang, Alexandra Birch, Chris C. Burch, Marcello Federico, Nicola Bertoldi, Brooke Cowan, Wade Shen, Christine Moran, Richard Zens, Chris Dyer, Ondrej Bojar, Alexandra Constantin, and Evan Herbst. 2007. Moses: Open source toolkit for statistical machine translation. In *ACL*. The Association for Computer Linguistics.

Alon Lavie and Abhaya Agarwal. 2007. Meteor: an automatic metric for mt evaluation with high levels of correlation with human judgments. In *Proceedings of the Second Workshop on Statistical Machine Translation*, StatMT '07, pages 228–231, Stroudsburg, PA, USA. Association for Computational Linguistics.

Nitin Madnani and Bonnie J. Dorr. 2010. Generating phrasal and sentential paraphrases: A survey of data-driven methods. *Computational Linguistics*, 36(3):341–387.

Nitin Madnani, Necip Fazil Ayan, Philip Resnik, and Bonnie J. Dorr. 2007. Using paraphrases for parameter tuning in statistical machine translation. In *Proceedings of the Second Workshop on Statistical Machine Translation*, StatMT '07, pages 120–127, Stroudsburg, PA, USA. Association for Computational Linguistics.

Daniel Marcu and William Wong. 2002. A phrase-based, joint probability model for statistical machine translation. In *Proceedings of the ACL-02 conference on Empirical methods in natural language processing - Volume 10*, EMNLP '02, pages 133–139, Stroudsburg, PA, USA. Association for Computational Linguistics.

Erwin Marsi and Emiel Krahmer. 2011. Construction of an aligned monolingual treebank for studying semantic similarity. (submitted for publication).

Franz J. Och and Hermann Ney. 2003. A systematic comparison of various statistical alignment models. *Comput. Linguist.*, 29(1):19–51, March.

Franz Josef Och and Hermann Ney. 2004. The alignment template approach to statistical machine translation. *Comput. Linguist.*, 30:417–449, December.

Franz J. Och, Christoph Tillmann, and Hermann Ney. 1999. Improved alignment models for Statistical Machine Translation. In *Proceedings of the Joint Workshop on Empirical Methods in NLP and Very Large Corpora*, pages 20–28, Maryland, USA.

Bo Pang, Kevin Knight, and Daniel Marcu. 2003. Syntax-based alignment of multiple translations: Extracting paraphrases and generating new sentences. In *HLT-NAACL*.

Chris Quirk, Chris Brockett, and William Dolan. 2004. Monolingual machine translation for paraphrase generation. In Dekang Lin and Dekai Wu, editors, *Proceedings of EMNLP 2004*, pages 142–149, Barcelona, Spain, July. Association for Computational Linguistics.

Siwei Shen, Dragomir R. Radev, Agam Patel, and Güneş Erkan. 2006. Adding syntax to dynamic programming for aligning comparable texts for the generation of paraphrases. In *Proceedings of the COLING/ACL 2006 Main Conference Poster Sessions*, pages 747–754, Sydney, Australia, July. Association for Computational Linguistics.

Yusuke Shinyama, Satoshi Sekine, Kiyoshi Sudo, and Ralph Grishman. 2002. Automatic paraphrase acquisition from news articles. In *Proceedings of Human Language Technology Conference (HLT 2002)*, pages 313–318, San Diego, USA.

Andreas Stolcke. 2002. SRILM - An Extensible Language Modeling Toolkit. In *In Proc. Int. Conf. on Spoken Language Processing*, pages 901–904, Denver, Colorado.

S. Vogel, Franz Josef Och, and Hermann Ney. 2000. The statistical translation module in the verbmobil system. In *KONVENS 2000 / Sprachkommunikation, Vortrge der gemeinsamen Veranstaltung 5. Konferenz zur Verarbeitung natrlicher Sprache (KONVENS), 6. ITG-Fachtagung "Sprachkommunikation"*, pages 291–293, Berlin, Germany, Germany. VDE-Verlag GmbH.

Sander Wubben, Antal van den Bosch, Emiel Krahmer, and Erwin Marsi. 2009. Clustering and matching headlines for automatic paraphrase acquisition. In E. Krahmer and M. Theune, editors, *The 12th European Workshop on Natural Language Generation*, pages 122–125, Athens. Association for Computational Linguistics.

Sander Wubben, Antal van den Bosch, and Emiel Krahmer. 2010. Paraphrase generation as monolingual translation: Data and evaluation. In B. Mac Namee J. Kelleher and I. van der Sluis, editors, *Proceedings of the 10th International Workshop on Natural Language Generation (INLG 2010)*, pages 203–207, Dublin.

Richard Zens, Franz Josef Och, and Hermann Ney. 2002. Phrase-based statistical machine translation. In *Proceedings of the 25th Annual German Conference on AI: Advances in Artificial Intelligence*, KI '02, pages 18–32, London, UK. Springer-Verlag.

Shiqi Zhao, Xiang Lan, Ting Liu, and Sheng Li. 2009. Application-driven statistical paraphrase generation. In *Proceedings of the Joint Conference of the 47th Annual Meeting of the ACL and the 4th International Joint Conference on Natural Language Processing of the AFNLP: Volume 2 - Volume 2*, ACL '09, pages 834–842, Stroudsburg, PA, USA. Association for Computational Linguistics.

Andreas Zollmann and Ashish Venugopal. 2006. Syntax augmented machine translation via chart parsing. In *Proceedings of the Workshop on Statistical Machine Translation*, StatMT '06, pages 138–141, Stroudsburg, PA, USA. Association for Computational Linguistics.

Text specificity and impact on quality of news summaries

Annie Louis
University of Pennsylvania
Philadelphia, PA 19104
lannie@seas.upenn.edu

Ani Nenkova
University of Pennsylvania
Philadelphia, PA 19104
nenkova@seas.upenn.edu

Abstract

In our work we use an existing classifier to quantify and analyze the level of specific and general content in news documents and their human and automatic summaries. We discover that while human abstracts contain a more balanced mix of general and specific content, automatic summaries are overwhelmingly specific. We also provide an analysis of summary specificity and the summary quality scores assigned by people. We find that too much specificity could adversely affect the quality of content in the summary. Our findings give strong evidence for the need for a new task in abstractive summarization: identification and generation of general sentences.

1 Introduction

Traditional summarization systems are primarily concerned with the identification of important and unimportant content in the text to be summarized. Placing the focus on this distinction naturally leads the summarizers to completely avoid the task of text-to-text generation and instead just select sentences for inclusion in the summary. In this work, we argue that the general and specific nature of the content is also taken into account by human summarizers; we show that this distinction is directly related to the quality of the summary and it also calls for the use and refinement of text-to-text generation techniques.

General sentences are overview statements. Specific sentences supply details. An example general and specific sentence from different parts of a news article are shown in Table 1.

[1] *The first shock let up as the eye of the storm moved across the city.*
[2] The National Hurricane Center in Miami reported its position at 2 a.m. Sunday at latitude 16.1 north, longitude 67.5 west, about 140 miles south of Ponce, Puerto Rico, and 200 miles southeast of Santo Domingo.

Table 1: General (in italics) and specific sentences

Prior studies have advocated that the distinction between general and specific content is relevant for text summarization. Jing and McKeown (2000) studied what edits people use to create summaries from sentences in the source text. Two of the operations they identify are *generalization* and *specification* where the source content gets changed in the summary with respect to specificity. In more recent work, Haghighi and Vanderwende (2009) built a summarization system based on topic models, where both topics at general document level as well as those at specific subtopic levels were learnt. The underlying idea here is that summaries are generated by a combination of content from both these levels. But since the preference for these two types of content is not known, Haghighi and Vanderwende (2009) use some heuristic proportions.

Many systems that deal with sentence compression (Knight and Marcu, 2002; McDonald, 2006; Galley and McKeown, 2007; Clarke and Lapata, 2008) and fusion (Barzilay and McKeown, 2005; Filippova and Strube, 2008), do not take into account the specificity of the original or desired sentence. However, Wan et al. (2008) introduce a generation task where a summary sentence is created by combining content from a key (general) sentence and its supporting sentences in the source. More recently, Marsi et al. (2010) manually annotated the transformations between source and compressed phrases and observe that *generalization* is a frequent transformation.

But it is not known what distribution of general and specific content is natural for summaries. In addition, an analysis of whether this aspect is related to quality of the summary has also not been done so far. We address this issue in our work, making use of an accurate classifier to identify general and specific sentences that we have developed (Louis and Nenkova, 2011).

We present the first quantitative analysis of general and specific content in a large corpus of news documents and human and automatic summaries produced for them. Our findings reveal that human-written abstracts have much more general content compared to human and system produced extractive summaries. We also provide an analysis of how this difference in specificity is related to aspects of summary quality. We show that too much specificity could adversely affect the quality of summary content. So we propose the task of creating general sentences for use in summaries. As a starting point in this direction, we discuss some insights into the identification and generation of general sentences.

2 Data

We obtained news documents and their summaries from the Document Understanding Conference (DUC) evaluations. We use the data from 2002 because they contain the three different types of summaries we wish to analyze—abstracts and extracts produced by people, and automatic summaries. For extracts, the person could only select complete sentences, without any modification, from the input articles. When writing abstracts people were free to write the summary in their own words.

We use data from the generic multi-document summarization task. There were 59 input sets, each containing 5 to 15 news documents on a topic. The task is to provide a 200 word summary. Two human-written abstracts and two extracts were produced for each input by trained assessors at NIST. Nine automatic systems participated in the conference that year and we have 524 automatic summaries overall.

3 General and specific sentences in news

Before we present our analysis of general and specific content in news summaries, we provide a brief description of our classifier and some example predictions. Our classifier is designed to predict for a given *sentence*, its class as general or specific.

As in our example in Table 1, a general sentence hints at a topic the writer wishes to convey but does not provide details. So a reader expects to see more explanation and specific sentences satisfy this role. We observed that certain properties are prominent in general sentences. They either express a strong sentiment, are vague or contain surprising content. Accordingly our features were based on word specificity, language models, length of syntactic phrases and the presence of polarity words. Just the words in the sentences were also a strong indicator of general or specific nature. But we found the combination of all non-lexical features to provide the best accuracy and is the setup we use in this work.

We trained our classifier on general and specific sentences from news texts. Initially, we utilized existing annotations of discourse relations as training data. This choice was based on our hypotheses that discourse relations such as exemplification relate a general with a specific sentence. Later, we verified the performance of the classifier on human annotated general and specific sentences, also from two genre of news articles, and obtained similar and accurate predictions. Detailed description of the features and training data can be found in Louis and Nenkova (2011).

Our classifier uses logistic regression and so apart from hard prediction into general/specific classes, we can also obtain a confidence (probability) measure for membership in a particular class. In our tests, we found that for sentences where there is high annotator agreement for placing in a particular class, the classifier also produces a high confidence prediction on the correct class. When the agreement was not high, the classifier confidence was lower. In this way, the confidence score indicates the level of general or specific content. So for our experiments in this paper, we choose to use the confidence score for a sentence belonging to a class rather than the classification decision.

The overall accuracy of the classifier in binary

[G1] "The crisis is not over".
[G2] No casualties have been reported, but experts are concerned that a major eruption could occur soon.
[G3] Seismologists said the volcano had plenty of built-up magma and even more severe eruptions could come later.
[G4] Their predictions might be a false alarm – the volcano may have done its worst already.
[S1] (These volcanoes – including Mount Lassen in Shasta County, and Mount Rainier and Mount St. Helens in Washington, all in the Cascade Range – arise where one of the earth's immense crust plates is slowly diving beneath another.); Pinatubo's last eruption, 600 years ago, is thought to have yielded at least as much molten rock – half a cubic kilometer – as Mount St. Helens did when it erupted in 1980.
[S2] The initial explosions on Mount Pinatubo at 8:51 a.m. Wednesday sent a 10-mile-high mushroom cloud of swirling ash and rock fragments into the skies over Clark Air Base, forcing the Air Force to evacuate hundreds of American volunteers who had stayed behind to guard it and to tend sensitive communications equipment.
[S3] Raymundo Punongbayan, director of the Philippine Institute of Vulcanology and Seismology, said Friday's blasts were part of a single eruption, the largest since Mount Pinatubo awoke Sunday from its 600-year slumber.

Table 2: General (G) and specific (S) sentences from input d073b

classification is 75%. More accurate predictions are made on the examples with high annotator agreement reaching over 90% accuracy on sentences where there was complete agreement between five annotators. So we expect the predictions from the classifier to be reliable for analysis in a task setting.

In Table 2, we show the top general and specific sentences (ranked by the classifier confidence) for one of the inputs, d073b, from DUC 2002. This input contains articles about the volcanic eruption at Mount Pinatubo. Here, the specific sentences provide a lot of details such as the time and impact of the eruption, information about previous volcanoes and about the people and organizations involved.

In the next section, we analyze the actual distribution of specific and general content in articles and their summaries for the entire DUC 2002 dataset.

4 Specificity analysis

For each text—input, human abstract, human extract and automatic summary—we compute a measure of specificity as follows. We use the classifier to mark for each sentence the confidence for belonging to the *specific* class. Each token in the text is assigned the confidence level of the sentence it belongs to. The *average specificity of words* is computed as the mean value of the confidence score over all the tokens.

The histogram of this measure for each type of text is shown in Figure 1.

For inputs, the average specificity of words ranges between 50 to 80% with a mean value of 65%. So, news articles tend to have more specific content than generic but the distribution is not highly skewed towards either of the extreme ends.

The remaining three graphs in Figure 1 represent the amount of specific content in summaries for the same inputs. Human abstracts, in contrast to the inputs, are spread over a wider range of specificity levels. Some abstracts have as low as 40% specificity and a few actually score over 80%. However, the sharper contrast with inputs comes from the large number of abstracts that have 40 to 60% specificity. This trend indicates that abstracts contain more general content compared to inputs. An unpaired two-sided t-test between the specificity values of inputs and abstracts confirmed that abstracts have significantly lower specificity. The mean value for abstracts is 62% while for inputs it is 65%.

The results of the analysis are opposite for human extracts and system summaries. The mean specificity value for human extracts is 72%, 10% higher compared to abstractive summaries for the same inputs. This difference is also statistically significant. System-produced summaries also show a similar trend as extracts but are even more heavily biased towards specific content. There are even examples of automatic summaries where the average specificity level reaches 100%. The mean specificity value is 74% which turned out significantly higher than all other types of texts, inputs and both types of human summaries. So system summaries appear to be overwhelmingly specific.

The first surprising result is the opposite characteristics of human abstracts and extracts. While abstracts tend to be more general compared to the input texts, extracts are more specific. Even though

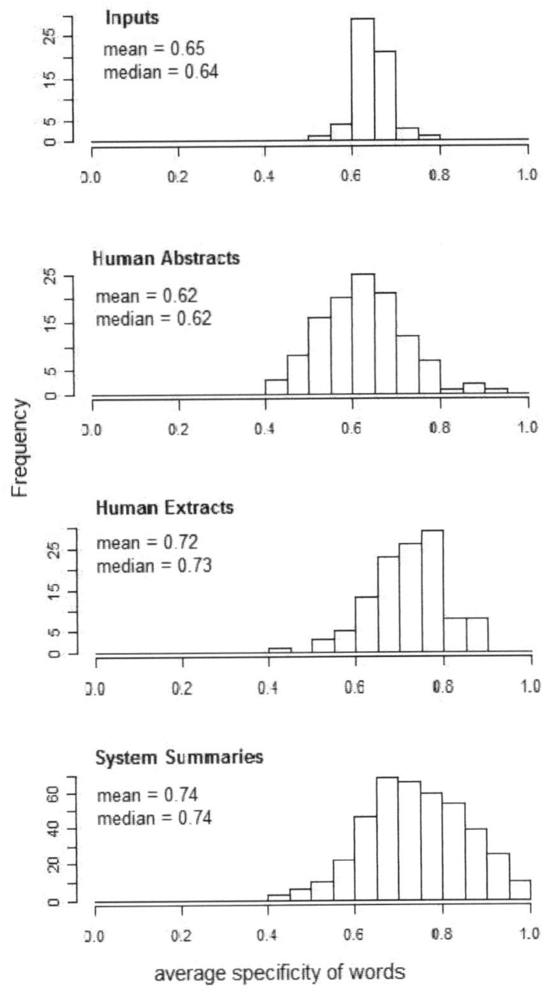

Figure 1: Specific content in inputs and summaries

both types of summaries were produced by people, we see that the summarization method deeply influences the nature of the summary content. The task of creating extractive summaries biases towards more specific content. So it is obvious that systems which mainly use extractive techniques would also create very specific summaries. Further, since high specificity arises as a result of the limitations associated with extractive techniques, perhaps, overly specific content would be detrimental to summary quality. We investigate this aspect in the next section.

5 Specificity and summary quality

In this section, we examine if the difference in specificity that we have observed is related to the perceived quality of the summary. Haghighi and Vanderwende (2009) report that their topic model based system was designed to use both a general content distribution and distributions of content for specific subtopics. However, using the general distribution yielded summaries with better content than using the specific topics. Here we directly study the relationship between specificity of system summaries and their content and linguistic quality scores. We also examine how the specificity measure is related to the quality of specialized summaries where people were explicitly told to include only general content or only specific details in their summaries. For this analysis, we focus on *system produced summaries*.

5.1 Content quality

At DUC, each summary is evaluated by human judges for content and linguistic quality. The quality of content was assessed in 2002 by means of a coverage score. The coverage score reflects the similarity between content chosen in a system summary and that which is present in a human-written summary for the same input. A human abstract is chosen as the reference. It is divided into clauses and for each of these clauses, judges decide how well it is expressed by the system produced summary (as a percentage value). The average extent to which the system summary expresses the clauses of the human summary is considered as the coverage score. So these scores range between 0 and 1.

We computed the Pearson correlation between the specificity of a summary and its coverage score, and obtained a value of -0.16. The correlation is not very high but it is significant (pvalue 0.0006). So specificity does impact content quality and more specific content indicates decreased quality.

We have seen from our analysis in the previous section that when people produce abstracts, they keep a mix of general and specific content but the abstracts are neither too general nor too specific. So it is not surprising that the correlation value is not very high. Further, it should be remembered that the notion of general and specific is more or less independent of the importance of the content itself. Two summaries can have the same level of generality but vary greatly in terms of the importance of the content present. So we performed an analysis to check the contribution of generality to the content scores in addition to the importance factor.

We combine a measure of content importance

Predictor	Mean β	Stdev. β	t value	p-value
(Intercept)	0.212	0.03	6.87	2.3e-11 *
rouge2	1.299	0.11	11.74	< 2e-16 *
avgspec	-0.166	0.04	-4.21	3.1e-05 *

Table 3: Results from regression test

ling score	sums.	avg specificity
1, 2	202	0.71
5	400	0.72
9, 10	79	0.77

Table 4: Number of summaries at extreme levels of linguistic quality scores and their average specificity values

from the ROUGE automatic evaluation (Lin and Hovy, 2003; Lin, 2004) with generality to predict the coverage scores. We use the same reference as used for the official coverage score evaluation and compute ROUGE-2 which is the recall of bigrams of the human summary by the system summary. Next we train a regression model on our data using the ROUGE-2 score and specificity as predictors of the coverage score. We then inspected the weights learnt in the regression model to identify the influence of the predictors. Table 3 shows the mean values and standard deviation of the beta coefficients. We also report the results from a test to determine if the beta coefficient for a particular predictor could be set to zero. The p-value for rejection of this hypothesis is shown in the last column and the test statistic is shown as the 't value'. We used the *lm* function in the R toolkit[1] to perform the regression.

From the table, we see that both ROUGE-2 and average specificity of words (avgspec) turn out as significant predictors of summary quality. Relevant content is highly important as shown by the positive beta coefficient for ROUGE-2. At the same time, it is preferable to maintain low specificity, a negative value is assigned to the coefficient for this predictor.

So too much specificity should be avoided by systems and we must find ways to increase the generality of summaries. We discuss this aspect in Sections 6 and 7.

5.2 Linguistic quality

We have seen from the above results that maintaining a good level of generality improves content quality. A related question is the influence of specificity on the linguistic quality of a summary. Does the amount of general and specific content have any relationship with how clear a summary is to read? We briefly examine this aspect here.

In DUC 2002 linguistic quality scores were only mentioned as the number of errors in a summary, not a holistic score. Moreover, it was specified as a range–errors between 1 and 5 receive the same score. So we use another dataset for this analysis only. We use the system summaries and their linguistic quality scores from the TAC '09 query focused summarization task[2]. Each summary was manually judged by NIST assessors and assigned a score between 1 to 10 to reflect how clear it is to read. The score combines multiple aspects of linguistic quality such as clarity of references, amount of redundancy, grammaticality and coherence.

Since these scores are on an integer scale, we do not compute correlations. Rather we study the specificity, computed in the same manner as described previously, of summaries at different score levels. Here there were 44 inputs and 55 systems. In Table 4, we show the number of summaries and their average specificity for 3 representative score levels—best quality (9 or 10), worst (1 or 2) and mediocre (5). We only used summaries with more than 2 sentences as it may not be reasonable to compare the linguistic quality of summaries of very short lengths.

From this table, we see that the summaries with greater score have a higher level of specificity. The specificity of the best summaries (9, 10) are significantly higher than that with medium and low scores (two-sided t-test). This result is opposite to our finding with content quality and calls attention to an important point. General sentences cannot stand alone and need adequate support and details. But currently, very few systems even make an attempt to organize their summaries. So overly general content and general content without proper context can be detrimental to the linguistic quality. Such summaries can appear uncontentful and difficult to read as the example in Table 5 demonstrates. This summary has an average specificity of 0.45 and its linguistic quality score is 1.

So we see an effect of specificity on both content

[1] http://www.r-project.org/

[2] http://www.nist.gov/tac/2009/Summarization/update.summ.09.guidelines.html

"We are quite a ways from that, actually."
As ice and snow at the poles melt, the loss of their reflective surfaces leads to exposed land and water absorbing more heat.
It is in the middle of an area whose population–and electricity demands–are growing.
It was from that municipal utility framework, city and school officials say, that the dormitory project took root.
"We could offer such a plan in Houston next year if we find customer demand, but we have n't gone to the expense of marketing the plan."
"We get no answers."

Table 5: Example general summary with poor linguistic quality

and linguistic quality though in opposite directions.

5.3 Quality of general and specific summaries

So far, we examined the effect of specificity on the quality of generic summaries. Now, we examine whether this aspect is related to the quality of summaries when they are optimized to be either general or specific content. We perform this analysis on DUC 2005[3] data where the task was to create a general summary for certain inputs. For others, a specific summary giving details should be produced. The definitions of a general and specific summary are given in the task guidelines.[4]

We tested whether the degree of specificity is related to the content scores[5] of system summaries of these two types—general and specific. The Pearson correlation values are shown in Table 6. Here we find that for specific summaries, the level of specificity is significantly positively correlated with content scores. For the general summaries there is no relationship between specificity and content quality.

These results show that specificity scores are not consistently predictive of distinctions within the *same* class of summaries. Within general summaries, the level of generality does not influence the scores obtained by them. This finding again highlights the disparity between content relevance and specific nature. When all summaries are specific or general, their levels of specificity are no longer indicative of quality. We also computed the regression models for these two sets of summaries with ROUGE scores and specificity, and specificity level was not a significant predictor of content scores.

Our findings in this section confirm that general sentences are useful content for summaries. So we face the issue of creating general sentences which are summary-worthy. We concentrate on this aspect for the rest of this paper. In Section 6, we provide an analysis of the types of general sentences extracted from the source text and used in human extracts. We move from this limited view and examine in Section 7, the possibility of generating general sentences from specific sentences in the source text. Our analysis is preliminary but we hope that it will initiate this new task of using general sentences for summary creation.

[3]http://duc.nist.gov/duc2005/

[4]http://duc.nist.gov/duc2005/assessor.summarization.instructions.pdf

[5]We use the official scores computed using the Pyramid evaluation method (Nenkova et al., 2007)

Summaries	**correlation**	**p-value**
DUC 2005 general	-0.03	0.53
DUC 2005 specific	0.18*	0.004

Table 6: Correlations between content scores and specificity for general and specific summaries in DUC 2005

6 Extraction of general sentences

We examine general sentences that were chosen in human extracts to understand what properties systems could use to identify such sentences from the source text. We show in Table 7, the ten extract sentences that were predicted to be general with highest confidence. The first sentence has a 0.96 confidence level, the last sentence has 0.81.

These statements definitely create expectation and need further details to be included. Taken out of context, these sentences do not appear very contentful. However despite the length restriction while creating summaries, humans tend to include these general sentences. Table 8 shows the full extract which contains one of the general sentences ([9] "Instead it sank like the Bismarck.").

When considered in the context of the extract, we see clearly the role of this general sentence. It introduces the topic of opposition to Bush's nomination for a defense secretary. Moreover, it provides a comparison between the ease with which such a proposition could have been accepted and the strikingly opposite situation that arose—the overwhelming rejection of the candidate by the senate. So sentence [9] plays the role of a topic sentence. It conveys the main point the author wishes to make in the summary and further details follow this sentence.

But given current content selection methods, such sentences would rank very low for inclusion into summaries. So the prediction of general sentences could prove a valuable task enabling systems to select good topic sentences for their summaries. However, proper ordering of sentences will be necessary to convey the right impact but this approach could be a first step towards creating summaries that have an overall theme rather than just the selection of sentences with important content.

We also noticed some other patterns in the general sentences chosen for extracts. A crude categorization was performed on the 75 sentences predicted with confidence above 0.65 and are shown below:

first sentence : 6 (0.08)
last sentence : 13 (0.17)
comparisons : 4 (0.05)
attributions : 14 (0.18)

A significant fraction of these general sentences (25%) were used in the extracts to start and end the summary, likely positions for topic sentences. Some of these (5%) involve comparisons. We detected these sentences by looking for the presence of connectives such as "but", "however" and "although". The most overwhelming pattern is presence of quotations, covering 18% of the sentences we examined. These quotations were identified using the words "say", "says", "said" and the presence of quotes. We can also see that three of the top 10 general sentences in Table 7 are quotes.

So far we have analyzed sentences chosen by summary authors directly from the input articles. In the next section, we analyze the edit operations made by people while creating abstractive summaries. Our focus is on the generalization operation where specific sentences are made general. Such a transformation would be the generation-based approach to obtain general sentences.

7 Generation of general sentences

We perform our analysis on data created for sentence compression. In this line of work (Knight and Marcu, 2002; McDonald, 2006; Galley and McKeown, 2007), compressions are learnt by analyzing pairs of sentences, one from the source text, the other from human-written abstracts such that they both have the same content. We use the sentence pairs available in the Ziff-Davis Tree Alignment corpus (Galley and McKeown, 2007). These sentences come from the Ziff-Davis Corpus (Harman and Liberman, 1993) which contains articles about technology products. Each article is also associated with an abstract. The alignment pairs are produced by allowing a limited number of edit operations to match a source sentence to one in the abstract. In this corpus, alignments are kept between pairs that have *any* number of deletions and upto 7 substitutions. There are 15964 such pairs in this data. It is worth noting that these limited alignments only map 25% of the abstract sentences, so they do not cover all the cases. Still, an analysis on this data could be beneficial to observe the trends.

[1] Folksy was an understatement.
[2] "Long live democracy"!
[3] The dogs are frequent winners in best of breed and best of show categories.
[4] Go to court.
[5] Tajikistan was hit most hard.
[6] Some critics have said the 16-inch guns are outmoded and dangerous.
[7] Details of Maxwell's death are sketchy.
[8] "Several thousands of people who were in the shelters and the tens of thousands of people who evacuated inland were potential victims of injury and death".
[9] Instead it sank like the Bismarck.
[10] "The buildings that collapsed did so because of a combination of two things: very poor soil and very poor structural design," said Peter I. Yanev, chairman of EQE Inc., a structural engineering firm in San Francisco.

Table 7: Example general sentences in humans extracts

We ran the classifier individually on each source sentence and abstract sentence in this corpus. Then we counted the number of pairs which undergo each transformation such as general-general, general-specific from the source to an abstract sentence. These results are reported in Table 9. The table also provides the average number of deletion and substitution operations associated with sentence pairs in that category as well as the length of the uncompressed sentence and the compression rate. Compression rate is defined as the ratio between the

Summary d118i-f:

- President-elect Bush designated Tower as his defense secretary on Dec. 16. [Specific]
- Tower's qualifications for the job –intelligence, patriotism and past chairmanship of the Armed Services Committee –the nomination should have sailed through with flying colors. [Specific]
- *Instead it sank like the Bismarck. [General]*
- In written testimony to the Senate panel on Jan. 26, Tower said he could "recall no actions in connection with any defense activities" in connection with his work for the U.S. subsidiary. [Specific]
- Tower has acknowledged that he drank excessively in the 1970s, but says he has reduced his intake to wine with dinner. [General]
- The Democratic-controlled Senate today rejected the nomination of former Texas Sen. John Tower as defense secretary, delivering a major rebuke to President Bush just 49 days into his term.[Specific]
- The Senate's 53-47 vote came after a bitter and divisive debate focused on Tower's drinking habits, behavior toward women and his business dealings with defense contractors. [General]

Table 8: Example extract with classifier predictions and a general sentence from Table 7

Type	Total	% total	Avg deletions	Avg subs.	Orig length	Compr. rate
SS	6371	39.9	16.3	3.9	33.4	56.6
SG	5679	35.6	21.4	3.7	33.5	40.8
GG	3562	22.3	9.3	3.3	21.5	60.8
GS	352	2.2	8.4	4.0	22.7	66.0

Table 9: Types of transformation of source into abstract sentences

length in words of the compressed sentence and the length of the uncompressed sentence. So lower compression rates indicate greater compression.

We find that the most frequent transformations are specific-specific (SS) and specific-general (SG). Together they constitute 75% of all transformations. But for our analysis, the SG transformation is most interesting. One third of the sentences in this data are converted from originally specific content to being general in the abstracts. So abstracts do tend to involve a lot of generalization.

Studying the SG transition in more detail, we can see that the original sentences are much longer compared to other transitions. This situation arises from the fact that specific sentences in this corpus are longer. In terms of the number of deletions, we see that both SS and SG involve more than 15 deletions, much higher than that performed on the general sentences. However, we do not know if these operations are proportional to the original length of the sentences. But looking at the compression rates, we get a clearer picture, the SG sentences after compression are only 40% their original length, the maximum compression seen for the transformation types. For GG and GS, about 60% of the original sentence words are kept. For the SG transition, long sentences are chosen and are compressed aggressively. In Table 10, we show some example sentence pairs undergoing the SG transition.

Currently, compression systems do not achieve the level of compression in human abstracts. Sentences that humans create are shorter than what systems produce. Our results predict that these could be the cases where specific sentences get converted into general. One reason why systems do not attain this compression level could be because they only consider a limited set of factors while compressing, such as importance and grammaticality. We believe that generality can be an additional objective which can be used to produce even shorter sentences which we have seen in our work, will also lead to summaries with better content.

8 Conclusion

In this work, we have provided the first quantitative analysis of general and specific content as relevant to the task of automatic summarization. We find that general content is useful for summaries however, current content selection methods appear to not include much general content. So we have proposed the task of identifying general content which could be used in summaries. There are two ways of achieving this—by identifying relevant general sentences from the input and by conversion from specific to

[1] American Mitac offers free technical support for one year at a toll-free number from 7:30 to 5:30 P.S.T.
American Mitac offers toll-free technical support for one year.
[2] In addition to Yurman, several other government officials have served on the steering committee that formed the group.
Several government officials also served on the steering committee.
[3] All version of the new tape drives, which, according to Goldbach, offer the lowest cost per megabyte for HSC-based 8mm tape storage, are available within 30 days of order.
The products are available within 30 days of order.
[4] In a different vein is Edward Tufte 's "The Visual Display of Quantitative Information" (Graphics Press, 1983), a book covering the theory and practice of designing statistical charts, maps, tables and graphics.
Tufte 's book covers the theory and practice of designing statistical charts, maps, tables and graphics.
[5] In addition, Anderson said two Ada 9X competitive procurements–a mapping and revision contract and an implementation and demonstration contract–will be awarded in fiscal 1990.
Two competitive procurements will be awarded in fiscal 1989.

Table 10: Example specific to general (in italics) compressions

general content. We have provided a brief overview of these two approaches.

Our work underscores the importance of compression and other post-processing approaches over extractive summaries. Otherwise system content could contain too much extraneous details which take up space where other useful content could have been discussed.

Our study also highlights a semantic view of summary creation. Summaries are not just a bag of important sentences as viewed by most methods today. Rather a text should have a balance between sentences which introduce a topic and those which discuss them in detail. So another approach to content selection could be the joint selection of a general sentence with its substantiation. In future work, it would be interesting to observe if such summaries are judged more responsive and of better linguistic quality than summaries which do not have such a structure.

References

R. Barzilay and K. McKeown. 2005. Sentence fusion for multidocument news summarization. *Computational Linguistics*, 31(3).

J. Clarke and M. Lapata. 2008. Global inference for sentence compression: An integer linear programming approach. *Journal of Artificial Intelligence Research*, 31(1):399–429.

K. Filippova and M. Strube. 2008. Sentence fusion via dependency graph compression. In *Proceedings of EMNLP*, pages 177–185.

M. Galley and K. McKeown. 2007. Lexicalized markov grammars for sentence compression. In *Proceedings NAACL-HLT*.

A. Haghighi and L. Vanderwende. 2009. Exploring content models for multi-document summarization. In *Proceedings of NAACL-HLT*, pages 362–370.

D. Harman and M. Liberman. 1993. Tipster complete. *Corpus number LDC93T3A, Linguistic Data Consortium, Philadelphia.*

H. Jing and K. McKeown. 2000. Cut and paste based text summarization. In *Proceedings of NAACL.*

K. Knight and D. Marcu. 2002. Summarization beyond sentence extraction: A probabilistic approach to sentence compression. *Artificial Intelligence*, 139(1).

C. Lin and E. Hovy. 2003. Automatic evaluation of summaries using n-gram co-occurrence statistics. In *Proceedings of HLT-NAACL.*

C. Lin. 2004. ROUGE: a package for automatic evaluation of summaries. In *ACL Text Summarization Workshop*.

A. Louis and A. Nenkova. 2011. General versus specific sentences: automatic identification and application to analysis of news summaries. Technical Report No. MS-CIS-11-07, University of Pennsylvania Department of Computer and Information Science.

E. Marsi, E. Krahmer, I. Hendrickx, and W. Daelemans. 2010. On the limits of sentence compression by deletion. In E. Krahmer and M. Theune, editors, *Empirical methods in natural language generation*, pages 45–66. Springer-Verlag, Berlin, Heidelberg.

R. McDonald. 2006. Discriminative sentence compression with soft syntactic evidence. In *EACL'06.*

A. Nenkova, R. Passonneau, and K. McKeown. 2007. The pyramid method: Incorporating human content selection variation in summarization evaluation. *ACM Trans. Speech Lang. Process.*, 4(2):4.

S. Wan, R. Dale, M. Dras, and C. Paris. 2008. Seed and grow: augmenting statistically generated summary sentences using schematic word patterns. In *Proceedings of EMNLP*, pages 543–552.

Towards Strict Sentence Intersection: Decoding and Evaluation Strategies

Kapil Thadani and **Kathleen McKeown**
Department of Computer Science
Columbia University
New York, NY 10027, USA
{kapil,kathy}@cs.columbia.edu

Abstract

We examine the task of strict sentence intersection: a variant of sentence fusion in which the output must only contain the information present in all input sentences and nothing more. Our proposed approach involves alignment and generalization over the input sentences to produce a generation lattice; we then compare a standard search-based approach for decoding an intersection from this lattice to an integer linear program that preserves aligned content while minimizing the disfluency in interleaving text segments. In addition, we introduce novel evaluation strategies for intersection problems that employ entailment-style judgments for determining the validity of system-generated intersections. Our experiments show that the proposed models produce valid intersections a majority of the time and that the segmented decoder yields advantages over the search-based approach.

1 Introduction

In recent years, there has been growing interest in text-to-text generation problems which transform text according to specifications. Tasks such as sentence compression, which strives to retain the most salient content of an input sentence, and sentence fusion, which attempts to combine the important content in related sentences, are useful components for tackling larger natural language problems such as abstractive summarization of documents. Systems for these types of text-to-text problems are typically evaluated on the informativeness of the output text as judged by human annotators.

A natural aspect of most text generation systems is that a given input can map to a range of lexically diverse outputs. However, text-to-text tasks defined with vague criteria such as the preservation of the "important" information in text can also permit outputs that are *semantically* distinct. This can make evaluation difficult; for instance, system-generated sentences may differ (partially or completely) in informational content from reference human-annotated text. This phenomenon has been noted and discussed in the task of pairwise sentence fusion (Daumé III and Marcu, 2004) and also in sentence compression (McDonald, 2006). Some examples are listed in Table 1.

In this work, we examine the task of *sentence intersection*: a variant of sentence fusion that does not permit semantic variation in the output. A strict[1] intersection system is expected to produce a fused sentence that contains all the information common to its input sentences and *avoid* information that is in just one of the inputs. In other words, a valid intersection should only contain information that is substantiated by all input sentences. The set-theoretic notions of intersection (along with union) have been employed to describe variants of sentence fusion tasks in previous work (Marsi and Krahmer, 2005; Krahmer et al., 2008) but, to our knowledge, this work is the first to explicitly tackle and evaluate the strict intersection task.

We focus on the case of unsupervised pairwise sentence intersection and propose a strategy to yield

[1]We use the term *strict* to make explicit the distinction from traditional fusion systems, which generally aim at notions of intersection but are not formally evaluated with respect to it.

(a) Fusion example from Daumé III and Marcu (2004)	(i) After years of pursuing separate and conflicting paths, AT&T and Digital Equipment Corp. agreed in June to settle their computer-to-PBX differences. (ii) The two will jointly develop an applications interface that can be shared by computers and PBXs of any stripe.
Human fusion #1	*AT&T and Digital Equipment Corp. agreed* in June to settle their computer-to-PBX differences and *develop an applications interface that can be shared by any computer or PBX.*
Human fusion #2	After years of pursuing different paths, *AT&T and Digital agreed to jointly develop an applications interface that can be shared by computers and PBXs of any stripe.*
(b) Compression example from McDonald (2006)	TapeWare , which supports DOS and NetWare 286 , is a value-added process that lets you directly connect the QA150-EXAT to a file server and issue a command from any workstation to back up the server
Human compression #1	*TapeWare* supports DOS and NetWare 286
Human compression #2 (hypothesized)	*TapeWare* lets you connect the QA150-EXAT to a file server

Table 1: Examples of text-to-text generation problems with multiple valid human-generated outputs that differ significantly in semantic content. Italicized text is used to indicate fragments that are semantically identical.

valid intersections that follows the basic framework of previous unsupervised fusion systems (Barzilay and McKeown, 2005; Filippova and Strube, 2008b). In our approach, the input sentences are first aligned using a modified version of a recent phrase-based alignment approach (MacCartney et al., 2008). We assume the alignments that are produced define aspects of the input that must appear in the output fusion and consider decoding strategies to recover intersections that preserve these alignments. In addition to a search-based decoding strategy, we propose a constrained integer linear programming (ILP) formulation that attempts to decode the most fluent sentence covering all these aspects while minimizing the size and disfluency of interleaving text. This is a fairly general model which can also be extended to other alignment-based tasks such as pairwise union and difference.

As this is a substantially more constrained task than generic sentence fusion, we also present a novel evaluation approach that avoids out-of-context salience judgments. We make use of a recently-released corpus of fusion candidates (McKeown et al., 2010) and propose a crowdsourced entailment-style evaluation to determine the *validity* of generated intersections, as well as the grammaticality of the sentences produced. Additionally, automated machine translation (MT) metrics are explored to quantify the amount of information missing from valid intersections. Our decoding strategies show promise under these experiments and we discuss potential directions for improving intersection performance.

2 Related Work

The distinction between intersection and union of text was introduced in the context of sentence fusion (Krahmer et al., 2008; Marsi and Krahmer, 2005) in order to distinguish between traditional fusion strategies that attempted to include only common content and fusions that attempted to include all non-redundant content from the input. We focus here on *strict* sentence intersection, explicitly incorporating a constraint that requires that a produced fusion must not contain information that is not present in all input sentences. This distinguishes our approach from traditional sentence fusion approaches (Jing and McKeown, 2000; Barzilay and McKeown, 2005; Filippova and Strube, 2008b) which generally attempt to retain common information but are typically evaluated in an abstractive summarization context in which additional information in the fusion output does not negatively impact judgments.

This task is also related to the field of sentence compression which has received much attention in recent years (Turner and Charniak, 2005; McDonald, 2006; Clarke and Lapata, 2008; Filippova and Strube, 2008a; Cohn and Lapata, 2009; Marsi et al., 2010). Intersections can be viewed as *guided* compressions in which the redundancy of information content across input sentences in a multidocument setting is assumed to directly indicate its salience, thereby consigning it to the output.

Additionally, in this work, we frequently consider the sentence intersection task from the perspective of textual entailment (cf. §5.1). The textual entailment task involves automatically determining whether a given hypothesis can be inferred from a textual premise (Dagan et al., 2005; Bar-Haim et al., 2006). Automatic construction of positive and negative entailment examples has been explored in the past (Bensley and Hickl, 2008) to provide training data for entailment systems; however the production of text that is simultaneously entailed by two (or more) sentences is a far more constrained and difficult challenge.

ILP has been used extensively for text-to-text generation problems in recent years (Clarke and Lapata, 2008; Filippova and Strube, 2008b; Woodsend et al., 2010), including techniques which incorporate syntax directly into the decoding to imporove the fluency of the resulting text. In this paper, we focus on generating valid intersections and do not incorporate syntactic and semantic constraints into our ILP models; these are areas we intend to explore in the future.

3 The Intersection Task

The need for strict variants of fusion is motivated by considerations of evaluation and utility in text-to-text generation tasks. Without explicit constraints on the semantic content of valid output, the operational definition of fusion can encompass the full spectrum from sentence intersection to sentence union. This makes the comparison of different fusion systems dependent on task-based utility[2]. In addition, intersection comprises an interesting problem in its own right. It necessitates the use of generalization over phrases in order to convey only the content of the input sentences when different wording is used and therefore involves more than just word deletion.

The analogy to set-theoretic intersection in this task implies an underlying consideration of each sentence as a set of informational concepts, similar to previous work in summarization and redundancy (Filatova and Hatzivassiloglou, 2004; Thadani and McKeown, 2008). While we don't commit to any semantic representation for such elements of information, we can nevertheless attempt to *identify* repeated information using well-studied natural language analysis techniques such as alignment and paraphrase recognition, and furthermore *isolate* this information through text-to-text generation techniques.

Consider, for example, the first sentence pair from the examples in Table 2. A valid intersection for these sentences must not contain any information that is not substantiated by both of them, so a fusion that mentions "Mr Litvinenko's poisoning", "Britain" or "Sunday" would not satisfy this criterion. In other words, a valid intersection must necessarily be textually entailed by every input sentence. Following this, we can interpret the sentence intersection task as one that requires the generation of fluent text that is *mutually entailed* by all input sentences[3]. We use this perspective in developing an evaluation technique for strict intersection in §5.1.

A major distinguishing factor between this work and previous work on fusion is that simply adding or deleting words in a sentence is not adequate; in many cases, intersections require additional words or phrases to be introduced in order to generalize over related but non-interchangeable aligned terms (such as "go" and "expand"). Additionally, we must attempt to avoid introducing additional content-bearing text in the output while simultaneously striving to maintain the fluency of text.

3.1 Dataset

A corpus of sentence fusion instances was recently made available by McKeown et al. (2010), consisting of 297 sentence pairs taken from newswire clusters and manually judged as being good candidates for fusion. Each sentence pair is accompanied by human-produced intersections and unions collected via Amazon's Mechanical Turk service[4]. McKeown et al. (2010) noted that union responses are mostly valid but intersections are frequently incorrect and

[2]For instance, systems may trade off conciseness against grammaticality, or informational content with degree of support across the input sentences.

[3]From this perspective, the complementary task of sentence union involves the generation of fluent text that entails all the input sentences.

[4]http://www.mturk.com

1	(i) Home Secretary John Reid said Sunday the inquiry would go wherever "the police take it." (ii) It comes as Home Secretary John Reid said the inquiry into Mr Litvinenko's poisoning would expand beyond Britain.
2	(i) Traces of polonium have been found on the planes on which they are believed to have travelled between London and Moscow. (ii) Small traces of radioactive substances had been found on the planes.
3	(i) Prosecutors allege that the accuser, who appeared in the program, was molested after the show aired. (ii) Prosecutors allege that the boy, a cancer survivor, was molested twice after the program aired.

Table 2: Example sentence pairs from the McKeown et al. (2010) corpus. Table 3 contains the corresponding system-generated intersections for these sentence pairs.

hypothesized that the task is more confusing for untrained annotators. A similar phenomenon was noted by Krahmer et al. (2008): while demonstrating that query-based human fusions exhibited less variation than generic fusions, it was also observed that intersections varied more than unions.

Due to the absence of adequate training data for intersection, our approach to the task is unsupervised, similar to previous work in fusion (Barzilay and McKeown, 2005; Filippova and Strube, 2008b) and sentence compression (Clarke and Lapata, 2008; Filippova and Strube, 2008a). Additionally, we focus on the case of pairwise sentence intersection and assume that the common information between the input sentence pair can be represented within a single output sentence. As a result, although the McKeown et al. (2010) corpus cannot be used for training an intersection model, we can make use of the sentence pairs it contains for evaluation.

4 Models for intersection

Our proposed strategies for sentence intersection involve phrase-based alignment, intermediate generalization steps that build a generation lattice and techniques for decoding an output sentence, as described below.

4.1 Phrase-based alignment

The alignment phase is a major component of any intersection system as it is used to uncover the common segments in the input that must be preserved in the output. We make use of an adaptation of the supervised MANLI phrase-based alignment technique originally developed for textual entailment systems (MacCartney et al., 2008); our implementation replaces approximate search-based decoding with exact ILP-based alignment decoding and incorporates syntactic constraints to produce more precise alignments (Thadani and McKeown, 2011). The aligner is trained on a corpus of human-generated alignment annotations produced by Microsoft Research (Brockett, 2007) for inference problems from the second Recognizing Textual Entailment (RTE2) challenge (Bar-Haim et al., 2006).

Entailment problems are inherently asymmetric because premise text is generally larger than hypothesis text; however, this does not apply to our intersection problems and consequently our MANLI implementation drops asymmetric indicator features. The absence of these features impacts alignment performance on RTE2 data but our reimplementation performs comparably to the original model under the alignment evaluation from MacCartney et al. (2008).

4.2 Ontology-based generalization

An aligned phrase pair produced by the previous step does not necessarily indicate that the phrases are equivalent but merely that they are similar in the given sentence context (such as "accuser" and "boy" in the third example from Table 2). We need to generalize over these phrases as they are not interchangeable from the perspective of the intersection task. We consider an alignment as containing three types of aligned phrases:

1. **Identical phrases or paraphrases:** Either of these may appear in the output
2. **Entailed phrases:** Only the entailed phrase must appear in a valid intersection
3. **Instances of a general concept:** The common concept must be lexicalized in the output

Although generalization of words within standalone sentences is usually hampered by word sense ambiguity, our approach is less likely to encounter this problem because we can generalize *simultaneously* over phrases which have already been aligned using additional information (such as their neighboring context), thus avoiding generalizations that do not fit the alignment.

For our experiments, we make use of the Wordnet ontology (Miller, 1995) to find the hypernyms common to every aligned pair of non-identical phrases, and only attempt to detect entailments which are comprised of specific instances that entail general concepts. This approach can be augmented by the use of entailment corpora and distributional clustering which we intend to explore in future work. We also use the lexical resource CatVar (Habash and Dorr, 2003) to try to generate morphological variants of aligned words that enable them to be interchanged without creating disfluencies.

4.3 Pragmatic abstraction

Our strategy assumes that aligned text must be preserved in output intersections whereas unaligned text must be minimized. However, unaligned text cannot simply be dropped as it may contain vital portions for generating fluent text. In addition, unaligned phrases can be caused by paraphrased or metaphorical text that the aligner is not capable of identifying. For example, the phrases "polonium" and "radioactive substances" in the second sentence pair from Table 2 fail to align with each other.

On the other hand, retaining unaligned text from one of the input sentences for the sake of fluency is likely to introduce information that is not supported by the other input sentence. We therefore need to abstract away as much content from the unaligned portions of the text as possible. For this purpose, we generate a large number of potential compressions and abstractions for every unaligned span that occurs between two consecutive aligned phrases in each sentence. These compressions and abstractions, referred to as *interleaving paths*, between pairs of aligned phrases essentially construct a lattice over the input sentences that encodes all potential intersection outputs.

Generation of interleaving paths is accomplished through the application of rules on the dependency parse structure over unaligned text spans from a single sentence (as well as spans that occur before the first aligned phrase and after the last aligned phrase in each sentence). Interleaving paths are generated by applying rules that:

1. Drop insignificant dependent words and unaligned prepositional phrases
2. Replace content-bearing verbs with tense-adjusted generic variants such as "did something" and "happened", with an exception for statement verbs
3. Replace nouns with generic words such as "someone" or "something", using Wordnet to determine which generic variant fits a noun
4. Suggest connective text fragments such as "something about" to cover long spans and clause boundaries

Our abstraction rules are relatively simple but can often generate reasonable interleaving paths. In general, we note that shorter abstractions are less likely to include glaring grammatical errors because long unaligned spans are often indicative of problematic alignments that either incorrectly relate unconnected terms or fail to recognize paraphrases.

4.4 Decoding strategies

After sentence alignment, generalization over aligned phrases and the construction of interleaving paths, we are left with a lattice that encodes potential intersections of the input sentence. Figure 1 describes the general structure of this lattice. Every alignment link encompasses a set of aligned phrases. Phrases may be identical or generalizations, in which case they can appear in the context of either sentence, or they may be sentence-specific (for example, verbs with different tenses or nominalizations like "nominated" and "nominations"). Additionally, the abstraction phase generates interleaving paths from unaligned spans between all pairs of alignment links. These paths are generated from individual sentences and can only be used to connect phrases that appear in the context of those sentences.

Our task now reduces to recovering a well-formed intersection from this lattice. We make use of a language model (LM) to judge fluency and propose two techniques to decode high-scoring text from the lattice: a simple beam-search technique and an ILP

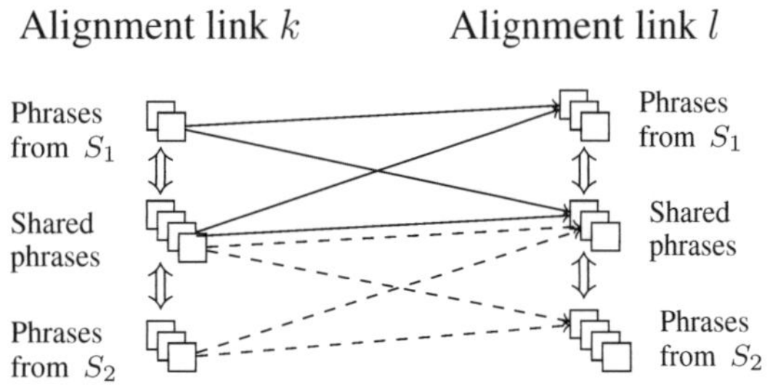

Figure 1: The general structure of one segment of the alignment lattice, illustrating the potential interleaving paths between aligned phrases. Solid lines indicate paths derived from sentence 1 and dashed lines indicate paths derived from sentence 2

strategy that leverages our initial assumption that all aligned phrases must appear in the output.

4.4.1 Beam search

Search-based decoding is often employed in phrase-based MT systems (Och and Ney, 2003) and is implemented in the Moses toolkit[5]; similar approaches have also been used in text-to-text generation tasks (Barzilay and McKeown, 2005; Soricut and Marcu, 2006). This technique attempts to find the highest-scoring sentence string under the LM by unwrapping and searching through a lattice. Since the dynamic programming search could require an exponential number of search states, a fixed-width beam can be used to control the number of search states being actively considered at each step.

In order to decode an intersection problem, we first pick a beam size B and initialize the list of candidate search states with the first interleaving paths in each sentence. At every iteration, we consider the B candidates with the highest normalized scores under the LM and remove them from the candidate list. Each candidate is then *advanced*, i.e., all aligned phrases and interleaving paths following it are examined, scored and added to the candidate list. We continue searching in this manner until B candidates have covered all aligned phrases; the highest scoring candidate is then retrieved as the target intersection.

4.4.2 Segmented decoding

While beam search is a viable strategy for decoding intersections, its performance is contingent on the beam size parameter and it is not guaranteed to return the highest scoring sentence under the LM. For instance, if a potential intersection starts with unusual text, it is unlikely to be explored by the search-based approach even if it is the optimal solution to the decoding problem. To address this, we also propose an alternative decoding problem that can be formulated as the optimization of a linear objective function with linear constraints. This can then be solved exactly by well-studied algorithms using off-the-shelf ILP solvers[6].

This decoding problem does not look for the highest scoring sentence under the LM; instead, it attempts to find the set of interleaving paths and aligned phrases that are most locally coherent[7] under the LM. Good phrase-path combinations that occur towards the tail end of an intersection can thus be put on even footing with the combinations that appear in the beginning. Although the two problems consider different objective functions, they are both engaged in the same overall goal: that of recovering a fluent sentence from the lattice.

We first define boolean indicator variables $a_i^k \in A_k$ for every aligned phrase in each aligned link A_k present in the intersection problem $\mathcal{I}$. We also introduce indicator variables p_{ij}^{kl} for every possible interleaving path between aligned phrases a_i^k and a_j^l. The linear objective for $\mathcal{I}$ that maximizes the local coherence of all phrases can be expressed as

$$f = \max \sum_{A_k, A_l \in \mathcal{I}} \sum_{i=0}^{|A_k|} \sum_{j=0}^{|A_l|} p_{ij}^{kl} \times score(p_{ij}^{kl})$$

where $score(p_{ij}^{kl})$ is the normalized LM score of the fragment of text representing $a_i^k \ p_{ij}^{kl} \ a_j^l$. In other words, the score for each interleaving path is calculated by appending it and the two phrases it connects into a single fragment of text and determining the score of that fragment under an LM[8].

[5] `http://www.statmt.org/moses/`

[6] We use LPsolve: `http://lpsolve.sourceforge.net/`

[7] As noted by Clarke and Lapata (2008), normalizing LM scores cannot be easily accomplished with linear constraints and we do not have training data to devise appropriate word-insertion penalties as used in MT.

[8] If the fragment of text is smaller than the LM size, we consider additional sentence context around the aligned phrases rather than backing off to a smaller LM size to avoid a bias towards short but ungrammatical interleaving paths.

We now introduce linear constraints to keep the problem well-formed. First, we add a restriction to ensure that only one phrase from each alignment link is present in the solution.

$$\sum_{a_i^k \in A_k} a_i^k = 1 \qquad \forall A_k \in \mathcal{I}$$

We can also ensure that interleaving paths are only in the solution when the aligned phrases that they connect together are themselves present using the following set of constraints.

$$a_i^k - \sum_{i=0}^{|A_k|} p_{i*}^{k*} = 1 \qquad \forall a_i^k \in A_k, A_k \in \mathcal{I}$$
$$a_j^l - \sum_{j=0}^{|A_l|} p_{*j}^{*l} = 1 \qquad \forall a_j^l \in A_l, A_l \in \mathcal{I}$$
$$p_{ij}^{kl} - a_i^k <= 0 \qquad \forall i, j, k, l$$
$$p_{ij}^{kl} - a_j^l <= 0 \qquad \forall i, j, k, l$$

As we don't restrict the structure of the lattice in any way and allow crossing alignment links, the program as defined thus far is capable of generating cyclic and fragmented solutions. To combat this, we add dummy start and end phrase variables and introduce additional *single commodity flow* constraints (Magnanti and Wolsey, 1994) adapted from Martins et al. (2009) over the interleaving paths to guarantee that the output will only involve a linear sequence of aligned phrases and paths.

5 Evaluation

We now turn to the design of experiments for the strict sentence intersection task and discuss the performance of the proposed models using the corpus provided by McKeown et al. (2010). We use a beam size of 50 for the beam search decoder and a 4-gram LM for all experiments. Dependency parsing is accomplished with MICA, a TAG-based parser (Bangalore et al., 2009). Our primary considerations for studying system-generated fusions are *validity* (whether the output contains only the information common to each sentence), *coverage* (whether the output contains all the common information in the input sentences) and the *fluency* of the output.

5.1 Evaluating Validity and Fluency

Evaluating the validity of an intersection involves determining whether it contains only the information contained in each sentence and nothing else. In order to do this, we make use of the interpretation of valid intersections as being mutually entailed by the input sentences. It follows that the task of judging the validity of an intersection can simply be decomposed into two tasks that judge whether the intersection is entailed by each input sentence.

We make use of Amazon's Mechanical Turk (AMT) platform to have humans evaluate the intersections produced. Crowdsourcing annotations and judgments in this manner has been shown to be cheap and effective for natural language tasks (Snow et al., 2008) and has recently been employed in similar entailment-detection tasks (Negri and Mehdad, 2010; Buzek et al., 2010). Since we only seek judgments on produced intersections and avoid presenting both input sentences to users, we do not anticipate the noisiness that was noted by McKeown et al. (2010) when asking AMT users to *generate* intersections.

Each entailment task is framed as a multiple choice question. An AMT user is shown just one input sentence (the *premise* in entailment terminology) along with a potential intersection (the *hypothesis*) and is required to respond to whether there is any new or different information in the latter that is not in the former. They can respond on a 3-point scale (*yes/no/maybe*) where *maybe* is clarified to include ambiguous rewording in the intersection. For a given intersection instance, the responses[9] using each input sentence as the premise are averaged separately and then combined[10] to give a measure of how well the intersection is entailed by *both* sentences.

A second question allows the user to specify the grammaticality of the intersection on a 4-point scale. As this measure doesn't depend on the input sentence presented to the AMT user, all scores provided are simply averaged per intersection.

[9]Each instance is presented to 6 AMT users, 3 per premise. Responses were automatically filtered for spam and removing the largest outlier from each per-premise or per-intersection group did not yield a notable change in relative performance.

[10]We use the harmonic mean for combination, but the results are largely similar when using an arithmetic mean.

	Intersection output	Fluency	Validity
Aligned words	(i) Home Secretary John Reid said the inquiry would go.	0.667	0.800
	(ii) Home Secretary John Reid said the inquiry would expand.	0.778	
Beam search	Home Secretary John Reid said something about the inquiry would move wherever "the something take it".	0.389	0.667
Segmented decoder	Home Secretary John Reid said the inquiry would change.	0.944	0.909
Aligned words	(i) Traces of have been found on the planes.	0.445	1.000
	(ii) traces of had been found on the planes.	0.556	
Beam search	Small traces of some things have been found on the planes.	0.611	0.909
Segmented decoder	Small traces of had been found on the planes.	0.500	0.741
Aligned words	(i) Prosecutors allege that the accuser the program was molested after aired.	0.167	0.800
	(ii) Prosecutors allege that the boy was molested after the program aired.	1.000	
Beam search	Prosecutors allege that the being, who did something in the program, was molested after something about aired.	0.400	0.909
Segmented decoder	Prosecutors allege that the organism, who did something, was molested after the program aired.	0.667	0.857

Table 3: Intersections produced for the examples introduced in Table 2 along with judgments from AMT users.

	Validity	Fluency	Har. Mean
Other sentence	0.188	0.945	0.314
Aligned words	0.863	0.563†	0.682†
Beam search	0.729	0.450	0.557
Segmented decoder	0.812†	0.504	0.622
Oracle combination	0.813†	0.575†	0.674†

Table 4: Results of the AMT evaluation described in §5.1. Statistically insignificant differences within columns are indicated with †; all other entries are significantly distinct at $p \leq 0.05$.

5.2 Results of AMT evaluation

Table 4 contains the results from this evaluation over the McKeown et al. (2010) corpus[11] and Table 3 shows the system-produced intersections corresponding to the examples from §3. We report normalized scores of validity and fluency for ease of comparison, as well as their unweighted harmonic mean as a crude measure of combined human judgment. In addition to the beam search and segmented decoders, we report the performance of two upper-bound systems that present artificial hypothesis sentences to AMT users. *Other sentence* is simply the sentence that is not the current premise from the sentence pair; although this is rarely an appropriate intersection in the data, it is useful as a measure of how well humans judge grammaticality and information content. *Aligned words* is the aligned subset of the premise sentence; this is quite likely to be considered a valid entailment by AMT users as no new words are introduced. Although the latter also scores surprisingly well on fluency, we must note that this is not an actual intersection solution: the aligned words displayed to AMT users for a given intersection instance are different depending on which input sentence is displayed as the premise.

Turning to the systems under study, we observe that the ILP-based segmented decoder produces text that is judged more fluent on average than the beam search decoder. In order to judge the degree of overlap between the two systems, we also report the performance of a pseudo-hybrid *oracle combination* system which assumes the presence of an oracle that runs both decoders and always chooses the output intersection that is more grammatical. The improved performance illustrates that each decoder has its advantages and that a real hybrid system might yield improvements over either approach.

5.3 Evaluating Coverage

While validity experiments test whether the proposed intersections contain extraneous or unsupported information, we also need to check whether the intersections contain *all* the information that is shared between the input sentences. This cannot be factored into a task that involves only one input sentence and therefore cannot be easily accomplished

[11]The first 20 sentence pairs of the corpus were examined when devising abstraction rules and are therefore excluded from these results.

	BLEU	NIST
Aligned words	0.682	11.10
Beam search	0.726	10.53
Segmented decoder	0.818	11.56

Table 5: Results of the automated evaluation for coverage of intersections described in §5.3.

without annotators who understand the concept of intersection.

We instead attempt to utilize the high-quality human-generated union dataset from McKeown et al. (2010) in evaluating the coverage of our intersection systems. Using the simple absorption law $A \cap (A \cup B) = A$, we assume that the coverage of intersection systems can be judged by how well they can recover an input sentence from human-generated unions. The resulting outputs are compared to the original input sentences in an MT-style evaluation under two commonly-used metrics: BLEU (Papineni et al., 2002) and NIST (Doddington, 2002).

The results of this automated evaluation are shown in Table 5. The *aligned words* system here always considers words from the union sentence and can therefore be seen as a baseline system. We observe that the segmented decoder produces output that is judged most similar to the input sentences under BLEU, which measures n-gram overlap, although results under NIST (which gives additional weight to *rarer* n-grams) are less conclusive.

6 Discussion

The experimental results indicate that the two systems we describe, particularly the segmented decoder, do a reasonable job of finding valid intersections with good coverage; however, producing fluent output remains a challenge. Analysis of the intersections produced leads us to note that the quality of interleaving paths is the prime obstacle to improving intersection output (cf. Table 3): producing syntactically-valid textual abstractions to connect text is a challenge that is not met by our simple rule-based approach. Furthermore, we notice that the quality of alignment also factors in to this problem: systems that miss phrases which should be aligned or systems that mistakenly align faraway fragments both cause spans of unaligned text that must be then abstracted over.

We hypothesize that these issues could be tackled with the use of joint models: a system that aligns as it decodes could reduce the need for abstraction over long unaligned spans, although care would have to be taken to ensure that coverage is maintained. Additionally, richer lexical resources such as wider-coverage ontologies (Snow et al., 2006) and entailment/paraphrase dictionaries could aid in improving coverage. Finally, previous work in fusion (Filippova and Strube, 2008b; Filippova and Strube, 2009) has noted that models based on syntax outperform techniques that rely solely on LM scores to determine fluency, and strict intersection appears to be well-suited for further exploration in this vein.

7 Conclusion

We have examined the text-to-text generation task of strict sentence intersection, which restricts semantic variation in the output and necessarily invokes the problems of generalization and abstraction in addition to the usual challenge of producing fluent text. We tackle the task as lattice decoding and discuss two decoding strategies for producing valid intersections. In addition, we assume that strict intersection tasks are best considered as problems of mutual entailment generation and describe evaluation strategies for this task that make use of both human judgments as well as automated metrics run over a related corpus. Experimental results indicate that these systems are fairly effective at generating valid intersections and that our novel segmented decoder strategy outperforms the traditional beam search approach. Although fluency remains a challenge, we hypothesize that the use of joint models, syntactic constraints and lexical resources could bring improvements.

Acknowledgments

The authors are grateful to the anonymous reviewers for their helpful feedback. This material is based on research supported in part by the U.S. National Science Foundation (NSF) under IIS-05-34871. Any opinions, findings and conclusions or recommendations expressed in this material are those of the authors and do not necessarily reflect the views of the NSF.

References

Srinivas Bangalore, Pierre Boullier, Alexis Nasr, Owen Rambow, and Benoît Sagot. 2009. MICA: a probabilistic dependency parser based on tree insertion grammars. In *Proceedings of HLT-NAACL: Short Papers*, pages 185–188.

Roy Bar-Haim, Ido Dagan, Bill Dolan, Lisa Ferro, Danilo Giampiccolo, Bernardo Magnini, and Idan Szpektor. 2006. The second PASCAL Recognising Textual Entailment challenge. In *Proceedings of the Second PASCAL Challenges Workshop on Recognising Textual Entailment*.

Regina Barzilay and Kathleen R. McKeown. 2005. Sentence fusion for multidocument news summarization. *Computational Linguistics*, 31(3):297–328.

Jeremy Bensley and Andrew Hickl. 2008. Unsupervised resource creation for textual inference applications. In *Proceedings of LREC*.

Chris Brockett. 2007. Aligning the 2006 RTE corpus. Technical Report MSR-TR-2007-77, Microsoft Research.

Olivia Buzek, Philip Resnik, and Benjamin B. Bederson. 2010. Error driven paraphrase annotation using mechanical turk. In *Proceedings of the NAACL HLT 2010 Workshop on Creating Speech and Language Data with Amazon's Mechanical Turk*, pages 217–221.

James Clarke and Mirella Lapata. 2008. Global inference for sentence compression: an integer linear programming approach. *Journal of Artifical Intelligence Research*, 31:399–429, March.

Trevor Cohn and Mirella Lapata. 2009. Sentence compression as tree transduction. *Journal of Artificial Intelligence Research*, 34:637–674.

Ido Dagan, Oren Glickman, and Bernardo Magnini. 2005. The pascal recognising textual entailment challenge. In *Proceedings of the PASCAL Challenges Workshop on Recognising Textual Entailment*.

Hal Daumé III and Daniel Marcu. 2004. Generic sentence fusion is an ill-defined summarization task. In *Proceedings of the ACL Text Summarization Branches Out Workshop*, pages 96–103.

George Doddington. 2002. Automatic evaluation of machine translation quality using n-gram co-occurrence statistics. In *Proceedings of HLT*, pages 138–145.

Elena Filatova and Vasileios Hatzivassiloglou. 2004. A formal model for information selection in multi-sentence text extraction. In *Proceedings of COLING*, page 397.

Katja Filippova and Michael Strube. 2008a. Dependency tree based sentence compression. In *Proceedings of the Fifth International Natural Language Generation Conference*, INLG '08, pages 25–32.

Katja Filippova and Michael Strube. 2008b. Sentence fusion via dependency graph compression. In *Proceedings of EMNLP*, pages 177–185.

Katja Filippova and Michael Strube. 2009. Tree linearization in English: improving language model based approaches. In *Proceedings of NAACL*, pages 225–228.

Nizar Habash and Bonnie Dorr. 2003. A categorial variation database for English. In *Proceedings of NAACL*, NAACL '03, pages 17–23.

Hongyan Jing and Kathleen R. McKeown. 2000. Cut and paste based text summarization. In *Proceedings of NAACL*, pages 178–185.

Emiel Krahmer, Erwin Marsi, and Paul van Pelt. 2008. Query-based sentence fusion is better defined and leads to more preferred results than generic sentence fusion. In *Proceedings of ACL*, pages 193–196.

Bill MacCartney, Michel Galley, and Christopher D. Manning. 2008. A phrase-based alignment model for natural language inference. In *Proceedings of EMNLP*, pages 802–811.

Thomas L. Magnanti and Laurence A. Wolsey. 1994. Optimal trees. In *Technical Report 290-94, Massechusetts Institute of Technology, Operations Research Center*.

Erwin Marsi and Emiel Krahmer. 2005. Explorations in sentence fusion. In *Proceedings of the European Workshop on Natural Language Generation*, pages 109–117.

Erwin Marsi, Emiel Krahmer, Iris Hendrickx, and Walter Daelemans. 2010. On the limits of sentence compression by deletion. In Emiel Krahmer and Mariët Theune, editors, *Empirical Methods in Natural Language Generation*, pages 45–66. Springer-Verlag, Berlin, Heidelberg.

André F. T. Martins, Noah A. Smith, and Eric P. Xing. 2009. Concise integer linear programming formulations for dependency parsing. In *Proceedings of ACL-IJCNLP*, pages 342–350.

Ryan McDonald. 2006. Discriminative sentence compression with soft syntactic evidence. In *Proceedings of EACL*, pages 297–304.

Kathleen McKeown, Sara Rosenthal, Kapil Thadani, and Coleman Moore. 2010. Time-efficient creation of an accurate sentence fusion corpus. In *Proceedings of NAACL-HLT*.

George A. Miller. 1995. Wordnet: a lexical database for english. *Communications of the ACM*, 38:39–41, November.

Matteo Negri and Yashar Mehdad. 2010. Creating a bi-lingual entailment corpus through translations with mechanical turk: $100 for a 10-day rush. In *Proceedings of the NAACL HLT 2010 Workshop on Creating*

Speech and Language Data with Amazon's Mechanical Turk, pages 212–216.

Franz Josef Och and Hermann Ney. 2003. A systematic comparison of various statistical alignment models. *Computational Linguistics*, 29:19–51, March.

Kishore Papineni, Salim Roukos, Todd Ward, and Wei-Jing Zhu. 2002. Bleu: a method for automatic evaluation of machine translation. In *Proceedings of ACL*, ACL '02, pages 311–318, Stroudsburg, PA, USA. Association for Computational Linguistics.

Rion Snow, Daniel Jurafsky, and Andrew Y. Ng. 2006. Semantic taxonomy induction from heterogenous evidence. In *Proceedings of ACL*, pages 801–808.

Rion Snow, Brendan O'Connor, Daniel Jurafsky, and Andrew Y. Ng. 2008. Cheap and fast—but is it good?: evaluating non-expert annotations for natural language tasks. In *Proceedings of EMNLP*, pages 254–263.

Radu Soricut and Daniel Marcu. 2006. Stochastic language generation using widl-expressions and its application in machine translation and summarization. In *Proceedings of ACL*, pages 1105–1112.

Kapil Thadani and Kathleen McKeown. 2008. A framework for identifying textual redundancy. In *Proceedings of COLING*, pages 873–880.

Kapil Thadani and Kathleen McKeown. 2011. Optimal and syntactically-informed decoding for monolingual phrase-based alignment. In *Proceedings of ACL*.

Jenine Turner and Eugene Charniak. 2005. Supervised and unsupervised learning for sentence compression. In *Proceedings of ACL*, pages 290–297.

Kristian Woodsend, Yansong Feng, and Mirella Lapata. 2010. Title generation with quasi-synchronous grammar. In *Proceedings of EMNLP*, EMNLP '10, pages 513–523.

Learning to Fuse Disparate Sentences

Micha Elsner
School of Informatics
University of Edinburgh
melsner0@gmail.com

Deepak Santhanam
Brown Lab for
Linguistic Information Processing (BLLIP)
Department of Computer Science
Brown University, Providence, RI 02912
dsanthan@microsoft.com

Abstract

We present a system for fusing sentences which are drawn from the same source document but have different content. Unlike previous work, our approach is supervised, training on real-world examples of sentences fused by professional journalists in the process of editing news articles. Like Filippova and Strube (2008), our system merges dependency graphs using Integer Linear Programming. However, instead of aligning the inputs as a preprocess, we integrate the tasks of finding an alignment and selecting a merged sentence into a joint optimization problem, and learn parameters for this optimization using a structured online algorithm. Evaluation by human judges shows that our technique produces fused sentences that are both informative and readable.

1 Introduction

Sentence fusion is the process by which content from two or more original sentences is transformed into a single output sentence. It is usually studied in the context of multidocument summarization, since fusing similar sentences can avoid repetition of material which is shared by more than one input. However, human editors and summarizers do not restrict themselves to combining sentences which share most of their content. This paper extends previous work on fusion to the case in which the input sentences are drawn from the same document and express fundamentally different content, while still remaining related enough to make fusion sensible[1].

Our data comes from a corpus of news articles for which we have un-edited and edited versions. We search this corpus for sentences which were fused (or separated) by the editor; these constitute naturally occurring data for our system. One example from our dataset consists of input sentences (1) and (2) and output (3). We show corresponding regions of the input and output in boldface.

(1) **The bodies showed signs of torture**.

(2) They **were left on the side of a highway in Chilpancingo, about an hour north of the tourist resort of Acapulco** in the southern state of Guerrero, **state police** said.

(3) **The bodies** of the men, which **showed signs of torture**, **were left on the side of a highway in Chilpancingo, which is about an hour north of the tourist resort of Acapulco**, **state police** told Reuters.

While the two original sentences are linked by a common topic and reference to a shared entity, they are not paraphrases of one another. This could create a problem for traditional fusion systems which first find an alignment between similar dependency graphs, then extract a shared structure. While our system has the same basic framework of alignment and extraction, it performs the two jointly, as parts of a global optimization task. This makes it robust to uncertainty about the hidden correspondences between the sentences. We use structured online learning to find parameters for the system, allowing it to

[1] Unfortunately, we cannot release our corpus due to licensing agreements. Our system is available at https://bitbucket.org/melsner/sentencefusion.

discover good ways to piece together input sentences by examining examples from our corpus.

Sentence fusion is a common strategy in human-authored summaries of single documents– 36% of sentences in the summaries investigated by Jing and McKeown (1999) contain content from multiple sentences in the original document. This suggests that a method to fuse dissimilar sentences could be useful for single-document summarization. Our dataset is evidence that editing also involves fusing sentences, and thus that models of this task could contribute to systems for automatic editing.

In the remainder of the paper, we first give an overview of related work (Section 2). We next describe our dataset and preprocessing in more detail (Section 3), describe the optimization we perform (Section 4), and explain how we learn parameters for it (Section 5). Finally, we discuss our experimental evaluation and give results (Section 6).

2 Related work

Previous work on sentence fusion examines the task in the context of multidocument summarization, targeting groups of sentences with mostly redundant content. The pioneering work on fusion is Barzilay and McKeown (2005), which introduces the framework used by subsequent projects: they represent the inputs by dependency trees, align some words to merge the input trees into a lattice, and then extract a single, connected dependency tree as the output.

Our work most closely follows Filippova and Strube (2008), which proposes using Integer Linear Programming (ILP) for extraction of an output dependency tree. ILP allows specification of grammaticality constraints in terms of dependency relationships (Clarke and Lapata, 2008), as opposed to previous fusion methods (Barzilay and McKeown, 2005; Marsi and Krahmer, 2005) which used language modeling to extract their output.

In their ILP, Filippova and Strube (2008) optimize a function based on syntactic importance scores learned from a corpus of general text. While similar methods have been used for the related task of sentence compression, improvements can be obtained using supervised learning (Knight and Marcu, 2000; Turner and Charniak, 2005; Cohn and Lapata, 2009) if a suitable corpus of compressed sentences can be obtained. This paper is the first we know of to adopt the supervised strategy for sentence fusion.

For supervised learning to be effective, it is necessary to find or produce example data. Previous work does produce some examples written by humans, though these are used during evaluation, not for learning (a large corpus of fusions (McKeown et al., 2010) was recently compiled as a first step toward a supervised fusion system). However, they elicit these examples by asking experimental subjects to fuse selected input sentences– the choice of which sentences to fuse is made by the system, not the subjects. In contrast, our dataset consists of sentences humans actually chose to fuse as part of a practical writing task. Moreover, our sentences have disparate content, while previous work focuses on sentences whose content mostly overlaps.

Input sentences with differing content present a challenge to the models used in previous work. All these models use deterministic node alignment heuristics to merge the input dependency graphs. Filippova and Strube (2008) align all content words with the same lemma and part of speech; Barzilay and McKeown (2005) and Marsi and Krahmer (2005) use syntactic methods based on tree similarity. Neither method is likely to work well for our data. Lexical methods over-align, since there are many potential points of correspondence between our sentences, only some of which should be merged– "the Doha trade round" and "U.S. trade representative" share a word, but probably ought to remain separate regardless. Syntactic methods, on the other hand, are unlikely to find any alignments since the input sentences are not paraphrases and have very different trees. Our system selects the set of nodes to merge during ILP optimization, allowing it to choose correspondences that lead to a sensible overall solution.

3 Data and preprocessing

Our sentence fusion examples are drawn from a corpus of 516 pre- and post-editing articles from the Thomson-Reuters newswire, collected over a period of three months in 2008. We use a simple greedy method based on bigram count overlaps to align the sentences of each original article to sentences in the edited version, allowing us to find fused sentences.

Since these sentences are relatively rare, we use both merges (where the editor fused two input sentences) and splits (where the editor splits an input sentence into multiple outputs) as examples for our system. In the case of a split, we take the edited sentences as input for our method and attempt to produce the original through fusion[2]. This is suboptimal, since the editor's decision to split the sentences probably means the fused version is too long, but is required in this small dataset to avoid sparsity.

Out of a total of 9007 sentences in the corpus, our bigram method finds that 175 were split and 132 were merged, for a total of 307. We take 92 examples for testing and 189 for training[3].

Following previous work (Barzilay and McKeown, 2005), we adopt a labeled dependency format for our system's input. To produce this, we segment sentences with MXTerminator (Reynar and Ratnaparkhi, 1997) and parse the corpus with the self-trained Charniak parser (McClosky et al., 2006). We then convert to dependencies and apply rules to simplify and label the graph. An example dependency graph is shown in Figure 1.

We augment the dependency tree by adding a potential dependency labeled "relative clause" between each subject and its verb. This allows our system to transform main clauses, like "the bodies showed signs of torture", into NPs like "the bodies, which showed signs of torture", a common paraphrase strategy in our dataset.

We also add correspondences between the two sentences to the graph, marking nodes which the system might decide to merge while fusing the two sentences. We introduce correspondence arcs between pairs of probable synonyms[4]. We also annotate pronoun coreference by hand and create a correspondence between each pronoun and the heads of all coreferent NPs. The example sentence has only a single correspondence arc ("they" and "bodies") because input sentence (1) is extremely short, but most sentences have more.

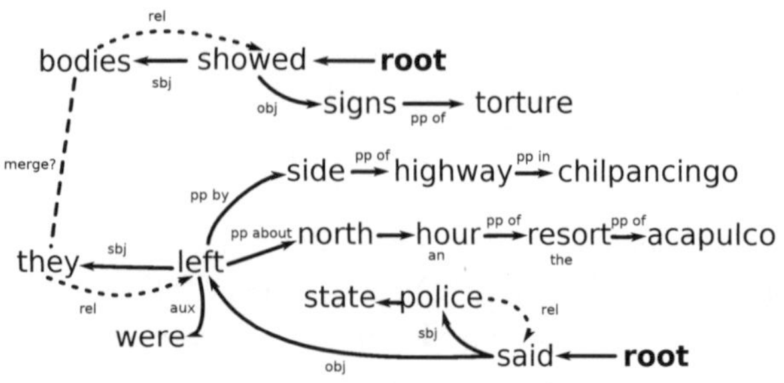

Figure 1: The labeled dependency graph for sentences (1) and (2). Dashed lines show a correspondence arc ("bodies" and "they") and potential relative clauses between subjects and VPs.

3.1 Retained information

Sentence fusion can be thought of as a two-part process: first, the editor decides which information from the input sentences to retain, and then they generate a sentence incorporating it. In this paper, we focus on the generation stage. To avoid having to perform content selection[5], we provide our system with the true information selected by the editor. To do this, we align the input sentences with the output by repeatedly finding the longest common substring (LCS) until a substring containing a matching content word can no longer be found. (The LCS is computed by a dynamic program similar to that for edit distance, but unlike edit distance, repeated LCS can handle reordering.) We provide our system with the boundaries of the retained regions as part of the input. For the example above, these are the regions of sentences (1) and (2) marked in boldface. Although this helps the system select the correct information, generating a grammatical and easy-to-read fused sentence is still non-trivial (see examples in section 7).

4 Fusion via optimization

Like Filippova and Strube (2008), we model our fusion task as a constrained optimization problem, which we solve using Integer Linear Programming (ILP). For each dependency from word w to head

[2] In a few cases, this creates two examples which share a sentence, since the editor sometimes splits content off from one sentence and merges it into another.

[3] We originally had 100 testing and 207 training examples, but found 26 of our examples were spurious, caused by faulty sentence segmentation.

[4] Words with the same part of speech whose similarity is greater than 3.0 according to the information-theoretic WordNet based similarity measure of Resnik (1995), using the implementation of (Pedersen et al., 2004).

[5] As pointed out by Daume III and Marcu (2004) and Krahmer et al. (2008), content selection is not only difficult, but also somewhat ill-defined without discourse context information.

h in the input sentences, we have a binary variable $x_{h,w}$, which is 1 if the dependency is retained in the output and 0 otherwise. However, unlike Filippova and Strube (2008), we do not know the points of correspondence between the inputs, only a set of possible points. Therefore, we also introduce 0-1 integer variables $m_{s,t}$ for each correspondence arc, which indicate whether word s in one sentence should be merged with word t in another. If the words are merged, they form a link between the two sentences, and only one of the pair appears in the output.

Each dependency x, each word w, and each merger m have an associated weight value v, which is assigned based on its features and the learned parameters of our system (explained in Section 5). Our objective function (4) sums these weight values for the structures we retain:

$$max \sum_{h,w} v_{h,w} \cdot v_w \cdot x_{h,w} + \sum_{s,t} v_{s,t} \cdot m_{s,t} \tag{4}$$

We use structural constraints to require the output to form a single connected tree. (In the following equations, W denotes the set of words, X denotes the set of dependencies and M denotes the potential correspondence pairs.) Constraint (5) requires a word to have at most one parent and (6) allows it to be merged with at most one other word. (7) and (8) require each merged node to have a single parent:

$$\forall w \in W, \sum_h x_{h,w} \leq 1 \tag{5}$$

$$\forall w \in W, \sum_t m_{s,t} \leq 1 \tag{6}$$

$$\forall s,t \in M, m_{s,t} \leq \sum_h x_{h,s} + \sum_h x_{h,t} \tag{7}$$

$$\forall s,t \in M, m_{s,t} + \sum_h x_{h,s} + \sum_h x_{h,t} \leq 2 \tag{8}$$

(9) forces the output to be connected by ensuring that if a node has children, it either has a parent or is merged.

$$\forall_w \in W, \sum_c x_{c,w} - |W| \sum_h x_{h,w} - |W| \sum_u m_{u,w} \leq 0 \tag{9}$$

Certain choices of nodes to merge or dependencies to follow can create a cycle, so we also introduce a rank variable $r_w \in \mathbb{R}$ for each word and constrain each word (except the root) to have a higher rank than its parent (10). Merged nodes must have equal ranks (11).

$$\forall_{w,h} \in X, |X| x_{h,w} + r_h - r_w \leq |X| - 1 \tag{10}$$

$$\forall_{s,t} \in M, |X| m_{s,t} + r_s - r_t \leq |X| \tag{11}$$

We also apply syntactic constraints to make sure we supply all the required arguments for each word we select. We hand-write rules to prevent the system from pruning determiners, auxiliary verbs, subjects, objects, verbal particles and the word "not" unless their head word is also pruned or it can find a replacement argument of the same type. We learn probabilities for prepositional and subclause arguments using the estimation method described in Filippova and Strube (2008), which counts how often the argument appears with the head word in a large corpus. While they use these probabilities in the objective function, we threshold them and supply constraints to make sure all argument types with probability $> 10\%$ appear if the head is chosen.

Word merging makes it more difficult to write constraints for required arguments, because a word s might be merged with some other word t which is attached to the correct argument type (for instance, if s and t are both verbs and they are merged, only one of them must be attached to a subject). This condition is modeled by the expression $m_{s,t} \cdot x_{t,a}$, where a is a argument word of the appropriate type. This expression is non-linear and cannot appear directly in a constraint, but we can introduce an auxiliary variable $g_{s,t,A}$ which summarizes it for a set of potential arguments A, while retaining a polynomial-sized program:

$$\forall_{s,t} \in M, \sum_{a \in A} x_{a,s} + \sum_{a \in A} x_{a,t} + |W| m_{s,t} - |W + 1| g_{s,t,A} \geq 0 \tag{12}$$

(13) then requires a word s to be connected to an argument in set A, either via a link or directly:

$$\sum_h x_{s,h} - 2 \sum_{t:\{s,t \in M\}} g_{s,t,A} - 2 \sum_{a \in A} x_{a,s} \leq 0 \quad (13)$$

The resulting resulting ILP is usually solvable within a second using CPLEX (Ilog, Inc., 2003).

4.1 Linearization

The output of the ILP is a dependency tree, not an ordered sentence. We determine the final ordering mostly according to the original word order of the input. In the case of a merged node, however, we must also interleave modifiers of the merged heads, which are not ordered with respect to one another. We use a simple heuristic, trying to place dependencies with the same arc label next to one another; this can cause errors. We must also introduce conjunctions between arguments of the same syntactic type; our system always inserts "and". Finally, we choose a realization for the dummy relative pronoun *THAT* using a trigram language model (Stolcke, 2002). A more sophisticated approach (Filippova and Strube, 2009) might lead to better results.

5 Learning

The solution which the system finds depends on the weights v which we provide for each dependency, word and merger. We set the weights based on a dot product of features ϕ and parameters α, which we learn from data using a supervised structured technique (Collins, 2002). To do so, we define a loss function $L(s, s') \rightarrow R$ which measures how poor solution s is when the true solution is s'. For each of our training examples, we compute the *oracle* solution, the best solution accessible to our system, by minimizing the loss. Finally, we use the structured averaged perceptron update rule to push our system's parameters away from bad solutions and towards the oracle solutions for each example.

Our loss function is designed to measure the high-level similarity between two dependency trees containing some aligned regions. (For our system, these are the regions found by LCS alignment of the input strings with the output.) For two sentences to be similar, they should have similar links between the regions. Specifically, we define the *paths* $P(s, C)$ in a tree s with a set of regions C as the set of word pairs w, w' where w is in one region, w' is in another, and the dependency path between w and w' lies entirely outside all the regions. An example is given in figure 2.

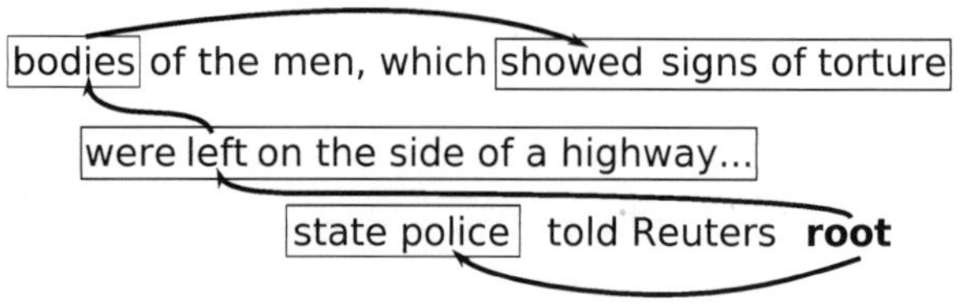

Figure 2: Paths between retained regions in sentence (3). Boxes indicate the retained regions.

Our loss (equation 14) is defined as the number of paths in s and s' which do not match, plus a penalty K_1 for keeping extra words, minus a bonus K_2 for retaining words inside aligned regions:

$$\begin{aligned} L(s,s';C,K) = \\ &|(P(s,C) \cup P(s',C)) \setminus (P(s,C) \cap P(s',C))| \\ &+ K_1|w \in s \setminus C| - K_2|w \in s \cap C| \end{aligned} \quad (14)$$

To compute the oracle s^*, we must minimize this loss function with respect to the human-authored reference sentence r over the space S of fused dependency trees our system can produce.

$$s^* = argmin_{s \in S} L(s, r) \quad (15)$$

We perform the minimization by again using ILP, keeping the constraints from the original program but setting the objective to minimize the loss. This cannot be done directly, since the existence of a path from s to t must be modeled as a product of x variables for the dependencies forming the path. However, we can again introduce a polynomial number of auxiliary variables to solve the problem. We introduce a 0-1 variable $q^s_{h,w}$ for each path start word s and dependency h, w, indicating whether the dependency from h to w is retained and forms part of a path from s. Likewise, we create variables q^s_w for each word and $q^s_{u,v}$ for mergers[6]. Using these variables, we can state the loss function linearly as (16),

[6]The q variables are constrained to have the appropriate values in the same way as (12) constrains g. We will print the specific equations in a technical report when this work is published.

where $P(r, C)$ is the set of paths extracted from the reference solution.

$$min \sum_{s,t} q^s_{h,t} - 2 \sum_{s,t \in P(r,C)} q^s_{h,t} \quad (16)$$

The oracle fused sentence for the example (1) and (2) is (17). The reference has a path from *bodies* to *showed*, so the oracle includes one as well. To do so, follows a relative clause arc, which was not in the original dependency tree but was created as an alternative by our syntactic analysis. (At this stage of processing, we show the dummy relative pronoun as *THAT*.) It creates a path from *left* to *bodies* by choosing to merge the pronoun *they* with its antecedent. Other options, such as linking the two original sentences with "and", are penalized because they would create erroneous paths– since there is no direct path between *root* and *showed*, the oracle should not make *showed* the head of its own clause.

(17) the bodies THAT showed signs of torture were left on the side of a highway in Chilpancingo about an hour north of the tourist resort of Acapulco state police said

The features which represent each merger, word and dependency are listed in Table 1. We use the first letters of POS tags (in the Penn Treebank encoding) to capture coarse groupings such as all nouns and all verbs. For mergers, we use two measures of semantic similarity, one based on Roget's Thesaurus (Jarmasz and Szpakowicz, 2003) and another based on WordNet (Resnik, 1995). As previously stated, we hand-annotate the corpus with true pronoun coreference relationships (about 30% of sentences contain a coreferent pronoun). Finally, we provide the LCS retained region boundaries as explained above.

Once we have defined the feature representation and the loss function, and can calculate the oracle for each datapoint, we can easily apply any structured online learning algorithm to optimize the parameters. We adopt the averaged perceptron, applied to structured learning by (Collins, 2002). For each example, we extract a current solution s_t by solving the ILP (with weights v dependent on our parameters α), then perform an update to α which forces the system away from s_t and towards the oracle solution s^*. The update at each timestep t (18) depends on the loss, the global feature vectors Φ, and

COMPONENT	FEATURES
MERGER	SAME WORD SAME POS TAGS SAME FIRST LETTER OF THE POS TAGS POS TAG IF WORD IS SAME COREFERENT PRONOUN SAME DEPENDENCY ARC LABEL TO PARENT ROGET'S SIMILARITY WORDNET SIMILARITY FIRST LETTER OF BOTH POS TAGS
WORD	POS TAG AND ITS FIRST LETTER WORD IS PART OF RETAINED CHUNK IN EDITOR'S FUSION
DEPENDENCY	POS TAGS OF THE PARENT AND CHILD FIRST LETTER OF THE POS TAGS TYPE OF THE DEPENDENCY DEPENDENCY IS AN INSERTED RELATIVE CLAUSE ARC PARENT IS RETAINED IN EDITOR'S SENTENCE CHILD IS RETAINED IN EDITOR'S SENTENCE

Table 1: List of Features.

a learning rate parameter η. (Note that the update leaves the parameters unchanged if the loss relative to the oracle is 0, or if the two solutions cannot be distinguished in terms of their feature vectors.)

$$\alpha_{t+1} = \alpha_t + \eta(L(s_t, r) - L(s^*, r))(\Phi(s^*) - \Phi(s_t)) \quad (18)$$

We do 100 passes over the training data, with η decaying exponentially toward 0. At the end of each pass over the data, we set $\hat{\alpha}$ to the average of all the α_t for that pass (Freund and Schapire, 1999). Finally, at the end of training, we select the committee of 10 $\hat{\alpha}$ which achieved lowest overall loss and average them to derive our final weights (Elsas et al., 2008). Since the loss function is nonsmooth, loss does not decrease on every pass, but it declines overall as the algorithm proceeds.

6 Evaluation

Evaluating sentence fusion is a notoriously difficult task (Filippova and Strube, 2008; Daume III and Marcu, 2004) with no accepted quantitative metrics, so we have to depend on human judges for evaluation. We compare sentences produced by our system to three alternatives: the editor's fused sentence, a readability upper-bound and a baseline formed by splicing the input sentences together by inserting the word "and" between each one. The readability upper bound is the output of parsing and linearization on the editor's original sentence (Filippova and Strube, 2008); it is designed to measure the loss in grammaticality due to our preprocessing.

Native English speakers rated the fused sentences with respect to readability and content on a scale of 1 to 5 (we give a scoring rubric based on (Nomoto, 2009)). 12 judges participated in the study, for a total of 1062 evaluations[7]. Each judge saw the each pair of inputs with the retained regions boldfaced, plus a single fusion drawn randomly from among the four systems. Results are displayed in Table 2.

System	Readability	Content
Editor	4.55	4.56
Readability UB	3.97	4.27
"And"-splice	3.65	3.80
Our System	3.12	3.83

Table 2: Results of human evaluation.

7 Discussion

Readability scores indicate that the judges prefer human-authored sentences, then the readability upper bound, then "and"-splicing and finally our system. This ordering is unsuprising considering that our system is abstractive and can make grammatical errors, while the remaining systems are all based on grammatical human-authored text. The gap of .58 between human sentences and the readability upper bound represents loss due to poor linearization; this accounts for over half the gap between our system and human performance.

For content, the human-authored sentences slightly outperform the readability upper bound–this indicates that poor linearization has some effect on content as well as readability. Our system is slightly better than "and"-splicing. The distribution of scores is shown in Table 3. The system gets more scores of 5 (perfect), but it occasionally fails drastically and receives a very low score; "and"-splicing shows less variance.

Both metrics show that, while our system does not achieve human performance, it does not lag behind by that much. It performs quite well on some relatively hard sentences and gets easy fusions right most of the time. For instance, the output on our example sentence is (19), matching the oracle (17).

	1	2	3	4	5	Total
"And"-splice	3	43	60	57	103	266
System	24	24	39	58	115	260

Table 3: Number of times each **Content** score was assigned by human judges.

(19) The bodies who showed signs of torture were left on the side of a highway in Chilpancingo about an hour north of the tourist resort of Acapulco state police said.

In some cases, the system output corresponds to the "and"-splice baseline, but in many cases, the "and"-splice baseline adds extraneous content. While the average length of a human-authored fusion is 34 words, the average splice is 49 words long. Plainly, editors often prefer to produce compact fusions rather than splices. Our own system's output has an average length of 33 words per sentence, showing that it has properly learned to trim away extraneous information from the input. We instructed participants to penalize the content score when fused sentences lost important information or added extra details.

Our integration of node alignment into our solution procedure helps the system to find good correspondences between the inputs. For inputs (20) and (21), the system was allowed to match "company" to "unit", but could also match "terrorism" to "administration" or to "lawsuit". Our system correctly merges "company" and "unit", but not the other two pairs, to form our output (22); the editor makes the same decision in their fused sentence (23).

(20) The suit **claims** the company **helped fly terrorism suspects abroad to secret prisons.**

(21) Holder's **review was disclosed the same day as Justice Department lawyers repeated a Bush administration** state-secret **claim in a lawsuit against a Boeing Co unit**.

[7]One judge completed only the first 50 evaluations; the rest did all 92.

(22) Review was disclosed the same day as Justice Department lawyers repeated a Bush administration claim in a lawsuit against a Boeing Co unit that helped fly terrorism suspects abroad to secret prisons.

(23) The review was disclosed the same day that Justice Department lawyers repeated Bush administration claims of state secrets in a lawsuit against a Boeing Co <BA.N> unit claiming it helped fly terrorism suspects abroad to secret prisons.

In many cases, even when the result is awkward or ungrammatical, the ILP system makes reasonable choices of mergers and dependencies to retain. For inputs (24) and (25), the system (26) decides "Secretary-General" belongs as a modifier on "de Mello", which is in fact the choice made by the editor (27). In order to add the relative clause, the editor paraphrased "de Mello's death" as "de Mello was killed". Our system, without this paraphrase option, is forced to produce the improper phrase "de Mello's death who"; a wider array of paraphrase options might lead to better results.

This example also demonstrates that the system does not simply keep the LCS-aligned retained regions and throw away everything else, since the result would be ungrammatical. Here it links the selected content by also choosing to keep "could have been", "an account" and "death".

(24) **Barker** mixes an account of **Vieira de Mello**'s death with scenes from his **career, which included working in countries such as Mozambique, Cyprus, Cambodia, Bangladesh, and the former Yugoslavia**.

(25) Had he lived, he could have been **a future U.N. Secretary-General.**

(26) Barker mixes an account of Vieira de Mello's death who could been a future U.N. secretary-general with scenes from career which included working in countries as such Mozambique Cyprus Cambodia and Bangladesh

(27) Barker recounted the day Vieira de Mello, a Brazilian who was widely tipped as a future U.N. Secretary-General, was killed and mixes in the story of the 55-year-old's career, which included working in countries such as Mozambique, Cyprus, Cambodia, Bangladesh, and Yugoslavia.

Many of our errors are due to our simplistic linearization. For instance, we produce a sentence beginning "Biden a veteran Democratic senator from Delaware that Vice president-elect and Joe...", where a correct linearization of the output tree would have begun "Vice President-elect Joe Biden, a veteran Democratic senator from Delaware that...". Some errors also occur during the ILP tree extraction process. In (28), the system fails to mark the arguments of "took" and "position" as required, leading to their omission, which makes the output ungrammatical.

(28) The White House that took when Israel invaded Lebanon in 2006 showed no signs of preparing to call for restraint by Israel and the stance echoed of the position.

8 Conclusion

We present a supervised method for learning to fuse disparate sentences. To the best of our knowledge, it is the first attempt at supervised learning for this task. We apply our method to naturally occurring sentences from editing data. Despite using text generation, our system is comparable to a non-abstractive baseline.

Our technique is general enough to apply to conventional fusion of similar sentences as well– all that is needed is a suitable training dataset. We hope to make use of the new corpus of McKeown et al. (2010) for this purpose. We are also interested in evaluating our approach on the fused sentences in abstractive single-document summaries.

The performance of our readability upper bound suggests we could improve our results using better tree linearization techniques and parsing. Although we show results for our system using hand-annotated pronoun coreference, it should be possible to use automatic coreference resolution instead.

Paraphrase rules would help our system replicate some output structures it is currently unable to match (for instance, it cannot convert between the copular "X is Y" and appositive "X, a Y" constructions). Currently, the system has just one such rule, which converts main clauses to relatives. Others could potentially be learned from a corpus, as in (Cohn and Lapata, 2009).

Finally, in this study, we deliberately avoid investigating the way editors choose which sentences to fuse and what content from each of them to retain. This is a challenging discourse problem that deserves further study.

Acknowledgements

We are very grateful to Alan Elsner, Howard Goller and Thomas Kim at Thomson-Reuters for giving us access to this dataset. We thank Eugene Charniak for his supervision, our colleagues in BLLIP for their comments, Kapil Thadani and Kathy McKeown for discussing the project with us, and our human evaluators for completing a task which turned out to be extremely tedious. Part of this work was funded by a Google Fellowship in Natural Language Processing.

References

Regina Barzilay and Kathleen McKeown. 2005. Sentence fusion for multidocument news summarization. *Computational Linguistics*, 31(3):297–328.

James Clarke and Mirella Lapata. 2008. Global inference for sentence compression: An integer linear programming approach. *J. Artif. Intell. Res. (JAIR)*, 31:399–429.

Trevor Cohn and Mirella Lapata. 2009. Sentence compression as tree transduction. *J. Artif. Intell. Res. (JAIR)*, 34:637–674.

Michael Collins. 2002. Discriminative training methods for hidden Markov models: Theory and experiments with perceptron algorithms. In *Proceedings of the 2002 Conference on Empirical Methods in Natural Language Processing*, pages 1–8. Association for Computational Linguistics, July.

Hal Daume III and Daniel Marcu. 2004. Generic sentence fusion is an ill-defined summarization task. In Stan Szpakowicz Marie-Francine Moens, editor, *Text Summarization Branches Out: Proceedings of the ACL-04 Workshop*, pages 96–103, Barcelona, Spain, July. Association for Computational Linguistics.

Jonathan L. Elsas, Vitor R. Carvalho, and Jaime G. Carbonell. 2008. Fast learning of document ranking functions with the committee perceptron. In *WSDM*, pages 55–64.

Katja Filippova and Michael Strube. 2008. Sentence fusion via dependency graph compression. In *Proceedings of the 2008 Conference on Empirical Methods in Natural Language Processing*, pages 177–185, Honolulu, Hawaii, October. Association for Computational Linguistics.

Katja Filippova and Michael Strube. 2009. Tree linearization in English: Improving language model based approaches. In *Proceedings of Human Language Technologies: The 2009 Annual Conference of the North American Chapter of the Association for Computational Linguistics, Companion Volume: Short Papers*, pages 225–228, Boulder, Colorado, June. Association for Computational Linguistics.

Yoav Freund and Robert E. Schapire. 1999. Large margin classification using the perceptron algorithm. *Machine Learning*, 37(3):277–296.

Ilog, Inc. 2003. Cplex solver.

Mario Jarmasz and Stan Szpakowicz. 2003. Roget's thesaurus and semantic similarity. In *Conference on Recent Advances in Natural Language Processing*, pages 212–219.

Hongyan Jing and Kathleen McKeown. 1999. The decomposition of human-written summary sentences. In *SIGIR*, pages 129–136.

Kevin Knight and Daniel Marcu. 2000. Statistics-based summarization - step one: sentence compression. In *Proceedings of the 17th National Conference on Artificial Intelligence*, pages 703–71.

Emiel Krahmer, Erwin Marsi, and Paul van Pelt. 2008. Query-based sentence fusion is better defined and leads to more preferred results than generic sentence fusion. In *Proceedings of ACL-08: HLT, Short Papers*, pages 193–196, Columbus, Ohio, June. Association for Computational Linguistics.

Erwin Marsi and Emiel Krahmer. 2005. Explorations in sentence fusion. In *Proceedings of the 10th European Workshop on Natural Language Generation*, pages 109–117.

David McClosky, Eugene Charniak, and Mark Johnson. 2006. Effective self-training for parsing. In *Proceedings of the Human Language Technology Conference of the NAACL, Main Conference*, pages 152–159.

Kathleen McKeown, Sara Rosenthal, Kapil Thadani, and Coleman Moore. 2010. Time-efficient creation of an accurate sentence fusion corpus. In *Human Language Technologies: The 2010 Annual Conference of the North American Chapter of the Association for Computational Linguistics*, pages 317–320, Los Angeles, California, June. Association for Computational Linguistics.

Tadashi Nomoto. 2009. A comparison of model free versus model intensive approaches to sentence compression. In *Proceedings of the 2009 Conference on Empirical Methods in Natural Language Processing*, pages 391–399, Singapore, August. Association for Computational Linguistics.

Ted Pedersen, Siddharth Patwardhan, and Jason Michelizzi. 2004. Wordnet::Similarity - measuring the relatedness of concepts. In Daniel Marcu Susan Dumais and Salim Roukos, editors, *HLT-NAACL 2004: Demonstration Papers*, pages 38–41, Boston, Massachusetts, USA, May 2 - May 7. Association for Computational Linguistics.

Philip Resnik. 1995. Using information content to evaluate semantic similarity in a taxonomy. In *IJCAI'95: Proceedings of the 14th international joint conference on Artificial intelligence*, pages 448–453, San Francisco, CA, USA. Morgan Kaufmann Publishers Inc.

Jeffrey C. Reynar and Adwait Ratnaparkhi. 1997. A maximum entropy approach to identifying sentence boundaries. In *Proceedings of the Fifth Conference on Applied Natural Language Processing*, pages 16–19, Washington D.C.

Andreas Stolcke. 2002. SRILM-an extensible language modeling toolkit. In *Proceedings of the International Conference on Spoken Language Processing*, pages 257–286, November.

Jenine Turner and Eugene Charniak. 2005. Supervised and unsupervised learning for sentence compression. In *Proc. Assoc. for Computational Linguistics (ACL)*, pages 290–297.

Framework for Abstractive Summarization using Text-to-Text Generation

Pierre-Etienne Genest, Guy Lapalme
RALI-DIRO
Université de Montréal
P.O. Box 6128, Succ. Centre-Ville
Montréal, Québec
Canada, H3C 3J7
{genestpe,lapalme}@iro.umontreal.ca

Abstract

We propose a new, ambitious framework for abstractive summarization, which aims at selecting the content of a summary not from sentences, but from an abstract representation of the source documents. This abstract representation relies on the concept of Information Items (INIT), which we define as the smallest element of coherent information in a text or a sentence. Our framework differs from previous abstractive summarization models in requiring a semantic analysis of the text. We present a first attempt made at developing a system from this framework, along with evaluation results for it from TAC 2010. We also present related work, both from within and outside of the automatic summarization domain.

1 Introduction

Summarization approaches can generally be categorized as extractive or abstractive (Mani, 2001). Most systems developped for the main international conference on text summarization, the Text Analysis Conference (TAC) (Owczarzak and Dang, 2010), predominantly use sentence extraction, including all the top-ranked systems, which make only minor post-editing of extracted sentences (Conroy et al., 2010) (Gillick et al., 2009) (Genest et al., 2008) (Chen et al., 2008).

Abstractive methods require a deeper analysis of the text and the ability to generate new sentences, which provide an obvious advantage in improving the focus of a summary, reducing its redundancy and keeping a good compression rate. According to a recent study (Genest et al., 2009b), there is an empirical limit intrinsic to pure extraction, as compared to abstraction. For these reasons, as well as for the technical and theoretical challenges involved, we were motivated to come up with an abstractive summarization model.

Recent abstractive approaches, such as sentence compression (Knight and Marcu, 2000) (Cohn and Lapata, 2009) and sentence fusion (Barzilay and McKeown, 2005) or revision (Tanaka et al., 2009) have focused on rewriting techniques, without consideration for a complete model which would include a transition to an abstract representation for content selection. We believe that a "fully abstractive" approach requires a separate process for the analysis of the text that serves as an intermediate step before the generation of sentences. This way, content selection can be applied to an abstract representation rather than to original sentences or generated sentences.

We propose the concept of *Information Items* (INIT) to help define the abstract representation. **An INIT is the smallest element of coherent information in a text or a sentence**. It can be something as simple as some entity's property or as complex as a whole description of an event or action. We believe that such a representation could eventually allow for directly answering queries or guided topic aspects, by generating sentences targeted to address specific information needs.

Figure 1 compares the workflow of our approach with other possibilities. Extractive summarization consists of selecting sentences directly from the

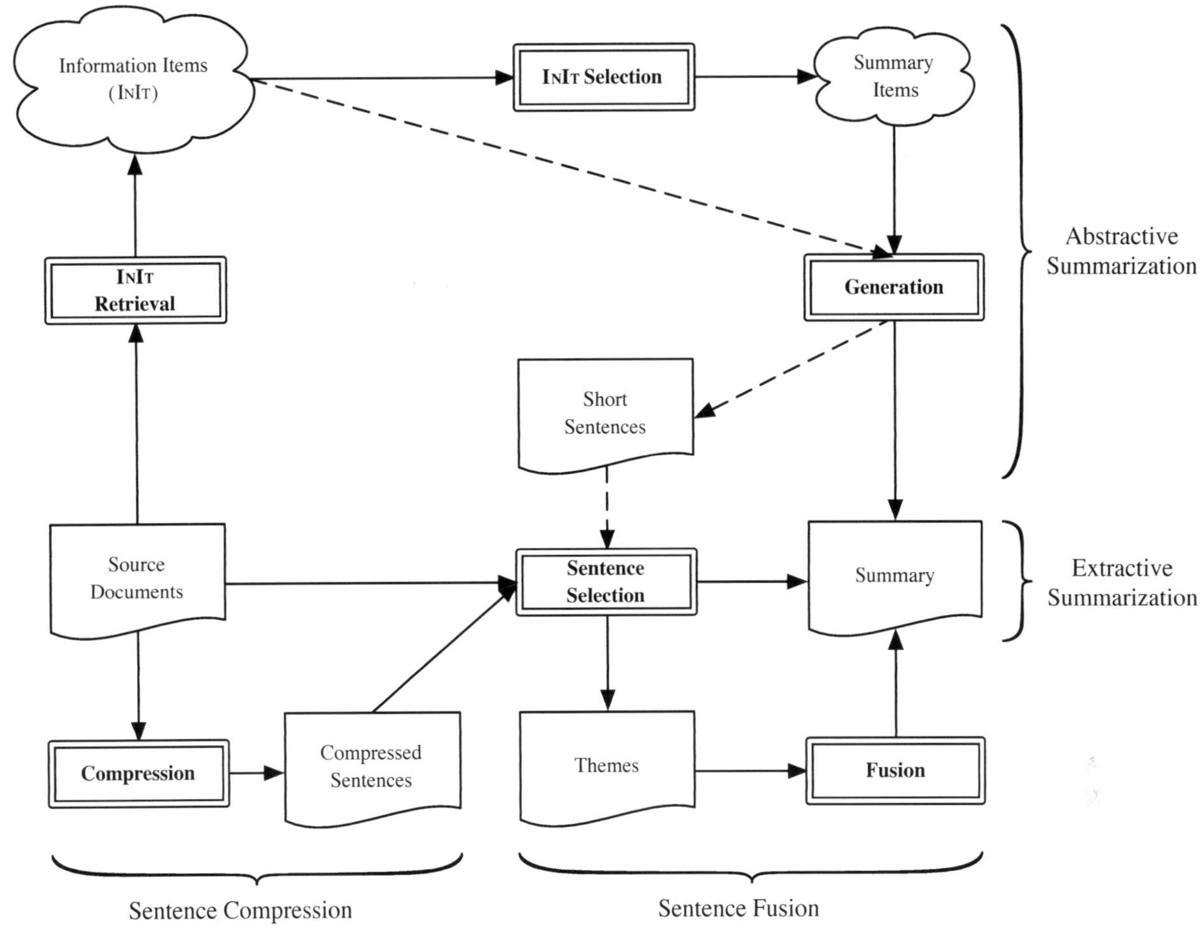

Figure 1: Workflow diagram of our suggested approach for abstractive summarization, compared to pure extractive summarization, sentence compression, and sentence fusion for summarization. The dashed line represents the simplified framework used in our first attempt at abstractive summarization (see section 2.4).

source documents and generating a summary from them. Sentence compression first compresses the sentences and chooses from those and the source documents' sentences to form a summary; it may also be completed in the reverse order, which is to select sentences from the source documents and then compress them for the summary. Sentence fusion first identifies themes (clusters of similar sentences) from the source documents and selects which themes are important for the summary (a process similar to the sentence selection of centroid-based extractive summarization methods (Radev et al., 2004)) and then generates a representative sentence for each theme by sentence fusion.

Our proposed abstractive summarization approach is fundamentally different because the selection of content is on Information Items rather than on sentences. The text-to-text generation aspect is also changed. Instead of purely going from whole sentences to generated sentences directly, there is now a text planning phase that occurs at the conceptual level, like in Natural Language Generation (NLG).

This approach has the advantage of generating typically short, information-focused sentences to produce a coherent, information rich, and less redundant summary. However, the difficulties are great: it is difficult for a machine to properly extract information from sentences at an abstract level, and text generated from noisy data will often be flawed. Generating sentences that do not all sound similar and generic is an additional challenge that we have for now circumvented by re-using the original sentence structure to a large extent, which is a type of text-to-text generation. Even considering those difficulties, we believe that efforts in abstractive summarization constitute the future of summarization research, and thus that it is worthwhile to work towards that end.

In this paper, we present our new abstractive summarization framework in section 2. Section 3 describes and analyses our first attempt at using this framework, for the TAC 2010 multi-document news summarization task, followed by the competition's results in section 4. In this first attempt, we simplified the framework of section 2 to obtain early results which can help us as we move forward in this project. Related work is discussed in section 5, and we conclude in section 6.

2 Abstractive Summarization Framework

Our proposed framework for fully abstractive summarization is illustrated in figure 1. This section discusses how each step could be accomplished.

2.1 INIT Retrieval

An Information Item is the smallest element of coherent information in a text or a sentence. This intentionally vague definition leaves the implementation details to be decided based on resources available. The goal is to identify all entities in the text, their properties, predicates between them, and characteristics of the predicates. This seemingly unreachable goal, equivalent to machine reading, can be limited to the extent that we only need INITs to be precise and accurate enough to generate a summary from them.

The implementation of INITs is critical, as everything will depend on the abstract information available. Semantic Role Labeling (SRL) and predicate-logic analysis of text are two potential candidates for developing INIT Retrieval. Word-sense disambiguation, co-reference resolution and an analysis of word similarity seem important as well to complement the semantic analysis of the text.

2.2 INIT Selection

Given an analysis of the source documents that leads to a list of INITs, we may now proceed to select content for the summary. Frequency-based models, such as those used for extractive summarization, could be applied to INIT selection instead of sentence selection. This would result in favoring the most frequently occurring entities, predicates, and properties.

INIT selection could also easily be applied to tasks such as query-driven or guided summarization, in which the user information need is known and the summarization system attempts to address it. With smaller building blocks (INITs rather than sentences), it would be much easier to tailor summaries so that they include only relevant information.

2.3 Generation

Planning, summary planning in our case, provides the structure of the generated text. Most INITs do not lead to full sentences, and need to be combined into a sentence structure before being realized as text. Global decisions of the INIT selection step now lead to local decisions as to how to present the information to the reader, and in what order.

Text generation patterns can be used, based on some knowledge about the topic or the information needs of the user. One could use heuristic rules with different priority levels or pre-generated summary scenarios, to help decide how to structure sentences and order the summary. We believe that machine learning could be used to learn good summary structures as well.

Once the detailed planning is completed, the summary is realized with coherent syntax and punctuation. This phase may involve text-to-text generation, since the source documents' sentences provide a good starting point to generate sentences with varied and complex structures. The work of (Barzilay and McKeown, 2005) on sentence fusion shows an example of re-using the same syntactical structure of a source sentence to create a new one with a slightly different meaning.

2.4 First Attempt at Abstractive Summarization

The three-step plan that we laid down is very hard, and instead of tackling it head on, we decided to focus on certain aspects of it for now. We followed a simplified version of our framework, illustrated by the dashed line in Figure 1. It defers the content selection step to the selection of generated short sentences, rather than actually doing it abstractly as

Original Sentence The Cypriot airliner that crashed in Greece may have suffered a sudden loss of cabin pressure at high altitude, causing temperatures and oxygen levels to plummet and leaving everyone aboard suffocating and freezing to death, experts said Monday.

Information Items

1. airliner – crash – *null* (Greece, August 15, 2005)
2. airliner – suffer – loss (Greece, August 15, 2005)
3. loss – cause – *null* (Greece, August 15, 2005)
4. loss – leave – *null* (Greece, August 15, 2005)

Generated Sentences

1. A Cypriot airliner crashed.
2. A Cypriot airliner may have suffered a sudden loss of cabin pressure at high altitude.
3. A sudden loss of cabin pressure at high altitude caused temperatures and oxygen levels to plummet.
4. A sudden loss of cabin pressure at high altitude left everyone aboard suffocating and freezing to death.

Selected Generated Sentence as it appears in the summary

1. On August 15, 2005, a Cypriot airliner crashed in Greece.

Original Sentence At least 25 bears died in the greater Yellowstone area last year, including eight breeding-age females killed by people.

Information Items

1. bear – die – *null* (greater Yellowstone area, last year)
2. person – kill – female (greater Yellowstone area, last year)

Generated Sentences

1. 25 bears died.
2. Some people killed eight breeding-age females.

Selected Generated Sentence as it appears in the summary

1. Last year, 25 bears died in greater Yellowstone area.

Figure 2: Two example sentences and their processing by our 2010 system. In the summary, the date and location associated with an INIT are added to its generated sentence.

planned. The summary planning has to occur after generation and selection, in a *Summary Generation* step not shown explicitly on the workflow.

We have restricted our implementation of INITs to dated and located subject–verb–object(SVO) triples, thus relying purely on syntactical knowledge, rather than including the semantics required for our framework. Dates and locations receive a special treatment because we were interested in news summarization for this first attempt, and news articles are factual and give a lot of importance to date and location.

We did not try to combine more than one INIT in the same sentence, relying instead on short, to-the-point sentences, with one INIT each. Figure 2 shows two examples of sentences that were generated from a source document sentence using the simplified abstractive summarization framework.

At first glance, the simplified version of our approach for generating sentences may seem similar to sentence compression. However, it differs in three important ways from the definition of the task of compression usually cited (Knight and Marcu, 2000):

- Our generated sentences intend to cover only one item of information and not all the important information of the original sentence.
- An input sentence may have several generated sentences associated to it, one for each of its INITs, where it normally has only one compressed sentence.
- Generated sentences sometimes include words that do not appear in the original sentence (like 'some' in the second example), whereas sentence compression is usually limited to word deletion.

3 Abstractive Summarization at TAC 2010

Our first attempt at full abstractive summarization took place in the context of the TAC 2010 multi-document news summarization task. This section describes briefly each module of our system, while (Genest and Lapalme, 2010) provides the implementation details.

3.1 INIT Retrieval

An INIT is defined as a dated and located subject–verb–object triple, relying mostly on syntactical analyses from the MINIPAR parser (Lin, 1998) and linguistic annotations from the GATE information extraction engine (Cunningham et al., 2002).

Every verb encountered forms the basis of a candidate INIT. The verb's subject and object are extracted, if they exist, from the parse tree. Each INIT is also tagged with a date and a location, if appropriate.

Many candidate INITs are rejected, for various reasons: the difficulty of generating a grammatical and meaningful sentence from them, the observed unreliability of parses that include them, or because it would lead to incorrect INITs most of the time. The rejection rules were created manually and cover a number of syntactical situations. Cases in which bad sentences can be generated remain, of course, even though about half the candidates are rejected. Examples of rejected Inits include those with verbs in infinitive form and those that are part of a conditional clause. Discarding a lot of available information is a significant limitation of this first attempt, which we will address as the first priority in the future.

3.2 Generation

From each INIT retrieved, we directly generate a new sentence, instead of first selecting INITs and planning the summary. This is accomplished using the original parse tree of the sentence from which the INIT is taken, and the NLG realizer SimpleNLG (Gatt and Reiter, 2009) to generate an actual sentence. Sample generated sentences are illustrated in Figure 2.

This process – a type of text-to-text generation – can be described as translating the parts that we want to keep from the dependency tree provided by the parser, into a format that the realizer understands. This way we keep track of what words play what role in the generated sentence and we select directly which parts of a sentence appear in a generated sentence for the summary. All of this is driven by the previous identification of INITs. We do not include any words identified as a date or a location in the sentence generation process, they will be generated if needed at the summary generation step, section 3.4.

Sentence generation follows the following steps:

- Generate a Noun Phrase (NP) to represent the subject if present
- Generate a NP to represent the object if present
- Generate a NP to represent the indirect object if present
- Generate a complement for the verb if one is present and only if there was no object
- Generate the Verb Phrase (VP) and link all the components together, ignoring anything else present in the original sentence

NP Generation

Noun phrase generation is based on the subtree of its head word in the dependency parse tree. The head in the subtree becomes the head of the NP and children in its parse subtree are added based on manual rules that determine which children are realized and how.

Verb Complement Generation

When an INIT has no object, then we attempt to find another complement instead, in case the verb would have no interesting meaning without a complement. The first verb modifier that follows it in the sentence order is used, including for example prepositional phrases and infinitive clauses.

VP Generation

Finally, the verb phrases are generated from each verb and some of its children. The NPs generated for the subject, object and indirect object are added, as well as the verb complement if it was generated. If there is an object but no subject, the VP is set to passive, otherwise the active form is always used. The tense (past or present) of the VP is set to the tense of the verb in the original sentence, and most modifiers like auxiliaries and negation are conserved.

3.3 Sentence Selection

To determine which of the generated sentences should be used in the summary, we would have liked to choose from among the INITs directly. For example, selecting the most frequent INIT, or INITs containing the most frequent subject-verb pair seem reasonable at first. However, during development, no such naive implementation of selecting INITs provided satisfactory results, because of the low frequency of those constructs, and the difficulty to compare them semantically in our current level of abstraction. Thus this critical content selection step occurs after the sentence generation process. Only the generated sentences are considered for the sentence selection process; original sentences from the source documents are ignored.

We compute a score based on the frequencies of the terms in the sentences generated from the INITs and select sentences that way. Document frequency (DF) – the number of documents that include an entity in its original text – of the lemmas included in the generated sentence is the main scoring criterion. This criterion is commonly used for summaries of groups of similar documents. The generated sentences are ranked based on their average DF (the sum of the DF of all the unique lemmas in the sentence, divided by the total number of words in the sentence). Lemmas in a stop list and lemmas that are included in a sentence already selected in the summary have their DF reduced to 0, to avoid favoring frequent empty words, and to diminish redundancy in the summary.

3.4 Summary Generation

A final summary generation step is required in this first attempt, to account for the planning stage and to incorporate dates and locations for the generated sentences.

Sentence selection provides a ranking of the generated sentences and a number of sentences intentionally in excess of the size limit of the summary is first selected. Those sentences are ordered by the date of their INIT when it can be determined. Otherwise, the day before the date of publication of the article that included the INIT is used instead. All generated sentences with the same known date are grouped in a single coordinated sentence. The date is included directly as a pre-modifier "On *date*," at the beginning of the coordination.

Each INIT with a known location has its generated sentence appended with a post-modifier "in *location*", except if that location has already been mentioned in a previous INIT of the summary.

At the end of this process, the size of the summary is always above the size limit. We remove the least relevant generated sentence and restart the summary generation process. We keep taking away the least relevant generated sentence in a greedy way, until the length of the summary is under the size limit. This naive solution to never exceed the limit was chosen because we originally believed that our INITs always lead to short generated sentences. However, it turns out that some of the generated summaries are a bit too short because some sentences that were removed last were quite long.

4 Results and Discussion

Here, we present and discuss the results obtained by our system in the TAC 2010 summarization system evaluation. We only show results for the evaluation of standard multi-document summaries; there was also an update task, but we did not develop a specific module for it. After ranking at or near the top with extractive approaches in past years (Genest et al., 2008) (Genest et al., 2009a), we expected a large drop in our evaluation results with our first attempt at abstractive summarization. In general, they are indeed on the low side, but mostly with regards to linguistic quality.

As shown in Table 1, the linguistic quality of our summaries was very low, in the bottom 5 of 43 participating automatic systems. This low linguistic score is understandable, because this was our first try at text generation and abstractive summarization, whereas the other systems that year used sentence extraction, with at most minor modifications made to the extracted sentences.

The cause of this low score is mostly our method for text generation, which still needs to be refined in several ways. The way we identify INITs, as we have already discussed, is not yet developped fully. Even in the context of the methodology outlined in section 3, and specifically 3.2, many improvements can still be made. Errors specific to the current state of our approach came from two major sources: incorrect parses, and insufficiently detailed and sometimes inappropriate rules for "translating" a part of a parse into generated text. A better parser would be helpful here and we will try other alternatives for dependency parsing in future work.

	Pyr.	Ling. Q.	Overall R.
AS	0.315	2.174	2.304
Avg	0.309	2.820	2.576
Best	0.425	3.457	3.174
Models	0.785	4.910	4.760
AS Rank	29	39	29

Table 1: Scores of pyramid, linguistic quality and overall responsiveness for our Abstractive Summarization (AS) system, the average of automatic systems (Avg), the best score of any automatic system (Best), and the average of the human-written models (Models). The rank is computed from amongst the 43 automatic summarization systems that participated in TAC 2010.

Although the linguistic quality was very low, our approach was given relatively good Pyramid (Nenkova et al., 2007) (a content metric) and overall responsiveness scores, near the average of automatic

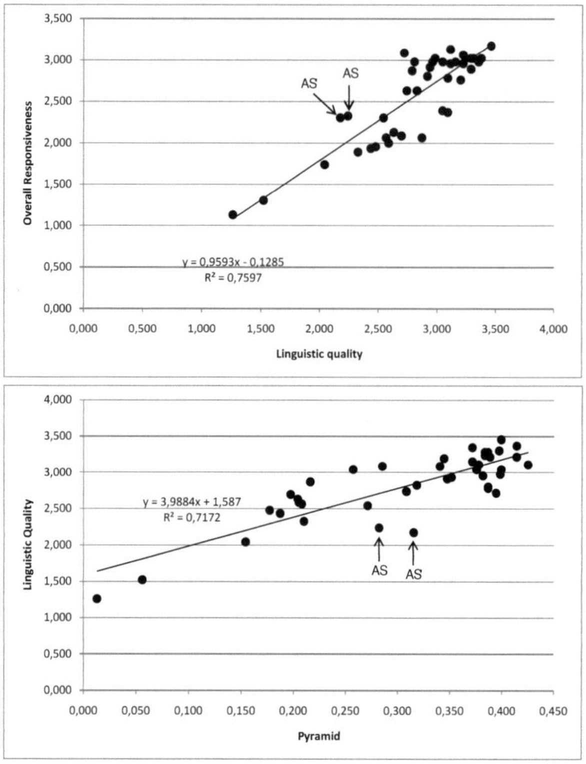

Figure 3: Scatter plots of overall responsiveness with respect to linguistic quality (top) and pyramid score with respect to linguistic quality (bottom), for all the systems competing in TAC 2010. The two runs identified with an arrow, AS and AS', were two similar versions of our abstractive summarization approach.

systems. This indicates that, even in a rough first try where content selection was not the main focus, our method is capable of producing summaries with reasonably good content and of reasonably good overall quality. There is a correlation between linguistic quality and the other two manual scores for most runs, but, as we can see in Figure 3, the two runs that we submitted stand out, even though linguistic quality plays a large role in establishing the overall responsiveness scores. We believe this to be representative of the great difference of our approach compared to extraction. By extension, following the trend, we hope that increasing the linguistic quality of our approach to the level of the top systems would yield content and overall scores above their current ones.

The type of summaries that our approach produces might also explain why it receives good content and overall scores, even with poor linguistic quality. The generated sentences tend to be short, and although some few may have bad grammar or even little meaning, the fact that we can pack a lot of them shows that INITS give a lot more flexibility to the content selection module than whole sentences, that only few can fit in a small size limit such as 100 words. Large improvements are to be expected, since this system was developped over only a few months, and we haven't implemented the full scale of our framework described in section 2.

5 Related Work

We have already discussed alternative approaches to abstractive summarization in the introduction. This section focuses on other work dealing with the techniques we used.

Subject–Verb–Object (SVO) extraction is not new. Previous work by (Rusu et al., 2007) deals specifically with what the authors call triplet extraction, which is the same as SVO extraction. They have tried a variety of parsers, including MINIPAR, and they build parse trees to extract SVOs similarly to us. They applied this technique to extractive summarization in (Rusu et al., 2009) by building what the authors call semantic graphs, derived from triplets, and then using said graphs to identify the most interesting sentences for the summary. This purpose is not the same as ours, and triplet extraction was conducted quite superficially (and thus included a lot of noise), whereas we used several rules to clean up the SVOs that would serve as INITS.

Rewriting sentences one idea at a time, as we have done in this work, is also related to the field of text simplification. Text simplification has been associated with techniques that deal not only with helping readers with reading disabilities, but also to help NLP systems (Chandrasekar et al., 1996). The work of (Beigman Klebanov et al., 2004) simplifies sentences by using MINIPAR parses as a starting point, in a process similar to ours, for the purpose of helping information-seeking applications in their own task. (Vickrey and Koller, 2008) applies similar techniques, using a sequence of rule-based simplifications of sentences, to preprocess documents for Semantic Role Labeling. (Siddharthan et al., 2004) uses shallow techniques for syntactical simplification of text by removing relative clauses and appositives, before running a sentence clustering algorithm for multi-document summarization.

The kind of text-to-text generation involved in our work is related to approaches in paraphrasing (Androutsopoulos and Malakasiotis, 2010). Paraphrase generation produces sentences with similar meanings, but paraphrase extraction from texts requires a certain level of analysis. In our case, we are interested both in reformulating specific aspects of a sentence, but also in identifying parts of sentences (INITS) with similar meanings, for content selection. We believe that there will be more and more similarities between our work and the field of paraphrasing as we improve on our model and techniques.

6 Conclusion

We have proposed an ambitious new way of looking at abstractive summarization, with our proposed framework. We believe that this framework aims at the real goals of automatic summarization – controlling the content and structure of the summary. This requires both an ability to correctly analyze text, and an ability to generate text. We have described a first attempt at fully abstractive summarization that relies on text-to-text generation.

We find the early results of TAC 2010 quite satisfactory. Receiving a low linguistic quality score was expected, and we are satisfied with average performance in content and in overall responsiveness. It means that our text-to-text generation was good enough to produce understandable summaries.

Our next step will be to go deeper into the analysis of sentences. Generating sentences should rely less on the original sentence structure and more on the information meant to be transmitted. Thus, we want to move away from the current way we generate sentences, which is too similar to rule-based sentence compression. At the core of moving toward full abstraction, we need to redefine INITS so that they can be manipulated (compared, grouped, realized as sentences, etc.) more effectively. We intend to use tools and techniques that will enable us to find words and phrases of similar meanings, and to allow the generation of a sentence that is an aggregate of information found in several source sentences. In this way, we would be moving away from purely syntactical analysis and toward the use of semantics.

References

Ion Androutsopoulos and Prodromos Malakasiotis. 2010. A survey of paraphrasing and textual entailment methods. *J. Artif. Int. Res.*, 38:135–187, May.

Regina Barzilay and Kathleen R. McKeown. 2005. Sentence fusion for multidocument news summarization. *Computational Linguistics*, 31(3):297–328.

Beata Beigman Klebanov, Kevin Knight, and Daniel Marcu. 2004. Text simplification for information-seeking applications. In Robert Meersman and Zahir Tari, editors, *Proceedings of Ontologies, Dabases, and Applications of Semantics (ODBASE) International Conference*, volume 3290 of *Lecture Notes in Computer Science*, pages 735–747, Agia Napa, Cyprus, October. Springer.

R. Chandrasekar, Christine Doran, and B. Srinivas. 1996. Motivations and methods for text simplification. In *Proceedings of the 16th conference on Computational linguistics - Volume 2*, COLING '96, pages 1041–1044, Stroudsburg, PA, USA. Association for Computational Linguistics.

Shouyuan Chen, Yuanming Yu, Chong Long, Feng Jin, Lijing Qin, Minlie Huang, and Xiaoyan Zhu. 2008. Tsinghua University at the Summarization Track of TAC 2008. In *Proceedings of the First Text Analysis Conference*, Gaithersburg, Maryland, USA. National Institute of Standards and Technology.

Trevor Cohn and Mirella Lapata. 2009. Sentence compression as tree transduction. *J. Artif. Int. Res.*, 34(1):637–674.

John M. Conroy, Judith D. Schlesinger, Peter A. Rankel, and Dianne P. O'Leary. 2010. CLASSY 2010: Summarization and metrics. In *Proceedings of the Third Text Analysis Conference*, Gaithersburg, Maryland, USA. National Institute of Standards and Technology.

Hamish Cunningham, Diana Maynard, Kalina Bontcheva, and Valentin Tablan. 2002. GATE: A framework and graphical development environment for robust NLP tools and applications. In *Proceedings of the 40th Annual Meeting of the Association for Computational Linguistics*, Philadelphia, PA, USA.

Albert Gatt and Ehud Reiter. 2009. SimpleNLG: a Realisation Engine for Practical Applications. In *ENLG '09: Proceedings of the 12th European Workshop on Natural Language Generation*, pages 90–93, Morristown, NJ, USA. Association for Computational Linguistics.

Pierre-Etienne Genest and Guy Lapalme. 2010. Text generation for abstractive summarization. In *Proceedings of the Third Text Analysis Conference*, Gaithersburg, Maryland, USA. National Institute of Standards and Technology.

Pierre-Etienne Genest, Guy Lapalme, Luka Nerima, and Eric Wehrli. 2008. A Symbolic Summarizer for the Update Task of TAC 2008. In *Proceedings of the First Text Analysis Conference*, Gaithersburg, Maryland, USA. National Institute of Standards and Technology.

Pierre-Etienne Genest, Guy Lapalme, Luka Nerima, and Eric Wehrli. 2009a. A symbolic summarizer with 2 steps of sentence selection for TAC 2009. In *Proceedings of the Second Text Analysis Conference*, Gaithersburg, Maryland, USA. National Institute of Standards and Technology.

Pierre-Etienne Genest, Guy Lapalme, and Mehdi Yousfi-Monod. 2009b. HexTac: the Creation of a Manual Extractive Run. In *Proceedings of the Second Text Analysis Conference*, Gaithersburg, Maryland, USA. National Institute of Standards and Technology.

David Gillick, Benoit Favre, Dilek-Hakkani Tür, Berndt Bohnet, Yang Liu, and Shasha Xie. 2009. The ICSI/UTD Summarization System at TAC 2009. In *Proceedings of the Second Text Analysis Conference*, Gaithersburg, Maryland, USA. National Institute of Standards and Technology.

Kevin Knight and Daniel Marcu. 2000. Statistics-based summarization - step one: Sentence compression. In *Proceedings of the Seventeenth National Conference on Artificial Intelligence and Twelfth Conference on Innovative Applications of Artificial Intelligence*, pages 703–710. AAAI Press.

Dekang Lin. 1998. Dependency-based evaluation of minipar. In *Proc. Workshop on the Evaluation of Parsing Systems*, Granada.

Inderjeet Mani. 2001. *Automatic Summarization*, volume 3 of *Natural Language Processing*. John Benjamins Publishing Company.

Ani Nenkova, Rebecca Passonneau, and Kathleen McKeown. 2007. The pyramid method: Incorporating human content selection variation in summarization evaluation. *ACM Trans. Speech Lang. Process.*, 4, May.

Karolina Owczarzak and Hoa Trang Dang. 2010. Overview of the TAC 2009 summarization track. In *Proceedings of the Third Text Analysis Conference*, Gaithersburg, Maryland, USA. National Institute of Standards and Technology. http://www.nist.gov/tac/publications/.

Dragomir R. Radev, Hongyan Jing, Malgorzata Stys, and Daniel Tam. 2004. Centroid-based summarization of multiple documents. *Information Processing and Management*, 40(6):919–938.

Delia Rusu, Lorand Dali, Blaz Fortuna, Marko Grobelnik, and Dunja Mladenic. 2007. Triplet extraction from sentences. *Proceedings of the 10th International Multiconference "Information Society – IS 2007"*, A:218–222, October.

Delia Rusu, Blaz Fortuna, Marko Grobelnik, and Dunja Mladenic. 2009. Semantic graphs derived from triplets with application in document summarization. *Informatica*, 33, October.

Advaith Siddharthan, Ani Nenkova, and Kathleen McKeown. 2004. Syntactic simplification for improving content selection in multi-document summarization. In *Proceedings of the 20th international conference on Computational Linguistics*, COLING '04, Stroudsburg, PA, USA. Association for Computational Linguistics.

Hideki Tanaka, Akinori Kinoshita, Takeshi Kobayakawa, Tadashi Kumano, and Naoto Kato. 2009. Syntax-driven sentence revision for broadcast news summarization. In *Proceedings of the 2009 Workshop on Language Generation and Summarisation*, UCNLG+Sum '09, pages 39–47, Stroudsburg, PA, USA. Association for Computational Linguistics.

David Vickrey and Daphne Koller. 2008. Sentence Simplification for Semantic Role Labeling. In *Proceedings of ACL-08: HLT*, pages 344–352, Columbus, Ohio, June. Association for Computational Linguistics.

Creating Disjunctive Logical Forms from Aligned Sentences for Grammar-Based Paraphrase Generation

Scott Martin and **Michael White**
Department of Linguistics
The Ohio State University
Columbus, Ohio, USA
{scott,mwhite}@ling.ohio-state.edu

Abstract

We present a method of creating disjunctive logical forms (DLFs) from aligned sentences for grammar-based paraphrase generation using the OpenCCG broad coverage surface realizer. The method takes as input word-level alignments of two sentences that are paraphrases and projects these alignments onto the logical forms that result from automatically parsing these sentences. The projected alignments are then converted into phrasal edits for producing DLFs in both directions, where the disjunctions represent alternative choices at the level of semantic dependencies. The resulting DLFs are fed into the OpenCCG realizer for n-best realization, using a pruning strategy that encourages lexical diversity. After merging, the approach yields an n-best list of paraphrases that contain grammatical alternatives to each original sentence, as well as paraphrases that mix and match content from the pair. A preliminary error analysis suggests that the approach could benefit from taking the word order in the original sentences into account. We conclude with a discussion of plans for future work, highlighting the method's potential use in enhancing automatic MT evaluation.

1 Introduction

In this paper, we present our initial steps towards merging the grammar-based and data-driven paraphrasing traditions, highlighting the potential of our approach to enhance the automatic evaluation of machine translation (MT). Kauchak and Barzilay (2006) have shown that creating synthetic reference sentences by substituting synonyms from Wordnet into the original reference sentences can increase the number of exact word matches with an MT system's output and yield significant improvements in correlations of BLEU (Papineni et al., 2002) scores with human judgments of translation adequacy. Madnani (2010) has also shown that statistical machine translation technique can be employed in a monolingual setting, together with paraphrases acquired using Bannard and Callison-Burch's (2005) pivot method, in order to enhance the tuning phase of training an MT system by augmenting a reference translation with automatic paraphrases. Earlier, Barzilay and Lee (2003) and Pang et al. (2003) developed approaches to aligning multiple reference translations in order to extract paraphrases and generate new sentences. By starting with reference sentences from multiple human translators, these data-driven methods are able to capture subtle, highly-context sensitive word and phrase alternatives. However, the methods are not particularly adept at capturing variation in word order or the use of function words that follow from general principles of grammar. By contrast, grammar-based paraphrasing methods in the natural language generation tradition (Iordanskaja et al., 1991; Elhadad et al., 1997; Langkilde and Knight, 1998; Stede, 1999; Langkilde-Geary, 2002; Velldal et al., 2004; Gardent and Kow, 2005; Hogan et al., 2008) have the potential to produce many such grammatical alternatives: in particular, by parsing a reference sentence to a representation that can be used as the input to a surface realizer, grammar-based paraphrases can be generated if the realizer supports n-best output. To our knowledge though, methods of using a grammar-based surface realizer together with multiple aligned reference sentences to produce synthetic

Source	Liu Lefei says that [in the long *term*] , in terms of *asset* allocation, overseas investment should occupy a certain *proportion* of [an insurance company's overall allocation] .
Reference	Liu Lefei said that in terms of *capital* allocation , outbound investment should make up a certain *ratio* of [overall allocations for insurance companies] [in the long *run*] .
Paraphrase	Liu Lefei says that [in the long *run*], in terms of *capital* allocation, overseas investment should occupy *the* certain *ratio* of an [insurance company's overall allocation]

Table 1: Zhao et al.'s (2009) similarity example, with italics added to show word-level substitutions, and square brackets added to show phrase location or construction mismatches. Here, the source sentence (itself a reference translation) has been paraphrased to be more like the reference sentence.

references have not been investigated.[1]

As an illustration of the need to combine grammatical paraphrasing with data-driven paraphrasing, consider the example that Zhao et al. (2009) use to illustrate the application of their paraphrasing method to similarity detection, shown in Table 1. Zhao et al. make use of a large paraphrase table, similar to the phrase tables used in statistical MT, in order to construct paraphrase candidates. (Like thesauri or WordNet, such resources are complementary to the ones we make use of here.) To test their system's ability to paraphrase reference sentences in service of MT evaluation, they attempt to paraphrase one reference translation to make it more similar to another reference translation; thus, in Table 1, the source sentence (itself a reference translation) has been paraphrased to be more like the (other) reference sentence. As indicated by italics, their system has successfully paraphrased *term*, *asset* and *proportion* as *run*, *capital* and *ratio*, respectively (though *the certain* seems to have been mistakenly substituted for *a certain*). However, their system is not capable of generating a paraphrase with *in the long run* at the end of the sentence, nor can it rephrase *insurance company's overall allocation* as *overall allocations for insurance companies*, which would seem to require access to more general grammatical knowledge.

To combine grammar-based paraphrasing with lexical and phrasal alternatives gleaned from multiple reference sentences, our approach takes advantage of the OpenCCG realizer's ability to generate from **disjunctive logical forms** (DLFs), i.e. packed semantic dependency graphs (White, 2004; White, 2006a; White, 2006b; Nakatsu and White, 2006; Espinosa et al., 2008; White and Rajkumar, 2009). In principle, semantic dependency graphs offer a better starting point for paraphrasing than the syntax trees employed by Pang et. al, as paraphrases can generally be expected to be more similar at the level of unordered semantic dependencies than at the level of syntax trees. Our method starts with word-level alignments of two sentences that are paraphrases, since the approach can be used with any alignment method from the MT (Och and Ney, 2003; Haghighi et al., 2009, for example) or textual inference (MacCartney et al., 2008, inter alia) literature in principle. The alignments are projected onto the logical forms that result from automatically parsing these sentences. The projected alignments are then converted into phrasal edits for producing DLFs in both directions, where the disjunctions represent alternative choices at the level of semantic dependencies. The resulting DLFs are fed into the OpenCCG realizer for n-best realization. In order to enhance the variety of word and phrase choices in the n-best lists, a pruning strategy is used that encourages lexical diversity. After merging, the approach yields an n-best list of paraphrases that contain grammatical alternatives to each original sentence, as well as paraphrases that mix and match content from the pair.

The rest of the paper is organized as follows. Section 2 provides background on surface realization with OpenCCG and DLFs. Section 3 describes our

[1]The task is not unrelated to sentence fusion in multidocument summarization (Barzilay and McKeown, 2005), except there the goal is to produce a single, shorter sentence from multiple related input sentences.

method of creating DLFs from aligned paraphrases. Finally, Section 4 characterizes the recurring errors and concludes with a discussion of related and future work.

2 Surface Realization with OpenCCG

OpenCCG is an open source Java library for parsing and realization using Baldridge's multimodal extensions to CCG (Steedman, 2000; Baldridge, 2002). In the chart realization tradition (Kay, 1996), the OpenCCG realizer takes logical forms as input and produces strings by combining signs for lexical items. Alternative realizations are scored using integrated n-gram and perceptron models (White and Rajkumar, 2009), where the latter includes syntactic features from Clark and Curran's (2007) normal form model as well as discriminative n-gram features (Roark et al., 2004). Hypertagging (Espinosa et al., 2008), or supertagging for surface realization, makes it practical to work with broad coverage grammars. For parsing, an implementation of Hockenmaier and Steedman's (2002) generative model is used to select the best parse. The grammar is automatically extracted from a version of the CCGbank (Hockenmaier and Steedman, 2007) with Propbank (Palmer et al., 2005) roles projected onto it (Boxwell and White, 2008).

A distinctive feature of OpenCCG is the ability to generate from disjunctive logical forms (White, 2006a). This capability has many benefits, such as enabling the selection of realizations according to predicted synthesis quality (Nakatsu and White, 2006), and avoiding repetition in the output of a dialogue system (Foster and White, 2007). Disjunctive inputs make it possible to exert fine-grained control over the specified paraphrase space. In the chart realization tradition, previous work has not generally supported disjunctive logical forms, with Shemtov's (Shemtov, 1997) more complex approach as the only published exception.

An example disjunctive input from the COMIC system appears in Figure 1(c).[2] Semantic dependency graphs such as these—represented internally in Hybrid Logic Dependency Semantics

[2] To simplify the exposition, the features specifying information structure and deictic gestures have been omitted, as have the semantic sorts of the discourse referents.

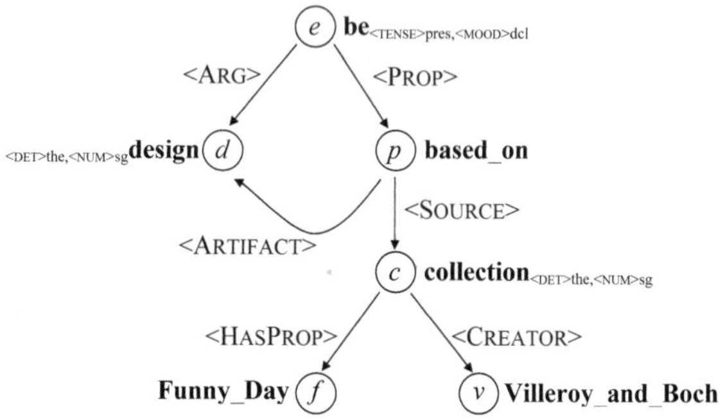

(a) Semantic dependency graph for *The design (is|'s) based on the Funny Day collection by Villeroy and Boch.*

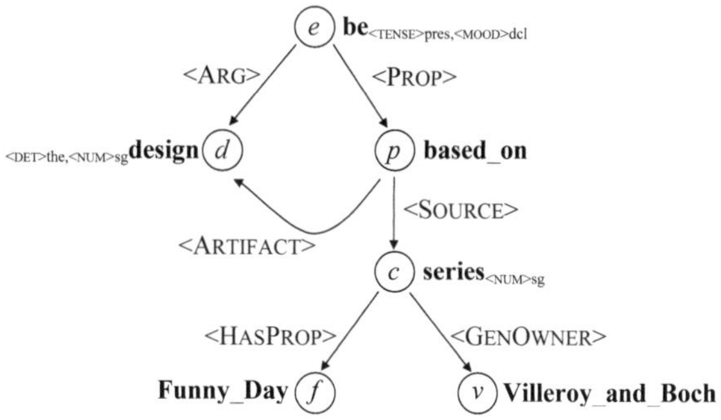

(b) Semantic dependency graph for *The design (is|'s) based on Villeroy and Boch's Funny Day series.*

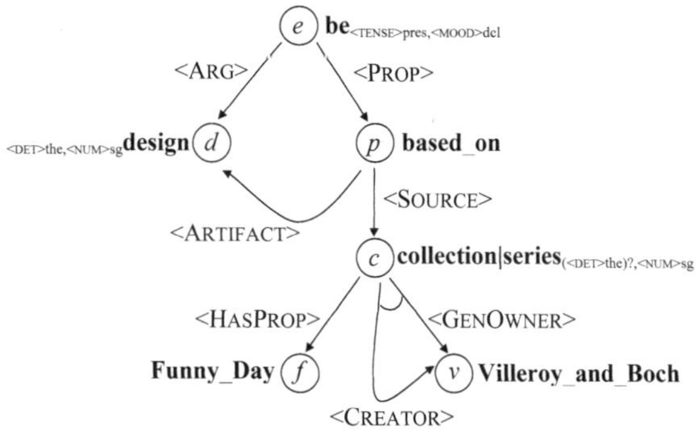

(c) Disjunctive semantic dependency graph covering (a)-(b), i.e. *The design (is|'s) based on (the Funny Day (collection|series) by Villeroy and Boch | Villeroy and Boch's Funny Day (collection|series)).*

Figure 1: Two similar logical forms from the COMIC system as semantic dependency graphs, together with a disjunctive logical form representing their combination as a packed semantic dependency graph.

(Baldridge and Kruijff, 2002; White, 2006b), or HLDS—constitute the input to the OpenCCG realizer.[3] This graph allows a free choice between the domain synonyms *collection* and *series*, as indicated by the vertical bar between their respective predications. The graph also allows a free choice between the ⟨CREATOR⟩ and ⟨GENOWNER⟩ relations—lexicalized via *by* and the possessive, respectively—connecting the head c (*collection* or *series*) with the dependent v (for *Villeroy and Boch*); this choice is indicated by an arc between the two dependency relations. Finally, the determiner feature (⟨DET⟩the) on c is indicated as optional, via the question mark. Note that as an alternative, the determiner feature could have been included in the disjunction with the ⟨CREATOR⟩ relation (though this would have been harder to show graphically); however, it is not necessary to do so, as constraints in the lexicalized grammar will ensure that the determiner is not generated together with the possessive.

3 Constructing DLFs from Aligned Paraphrases

To develop our approach, we use the gold-standard alignments in Cohn et al.'s (2008) paraphrase corpus. This corpus is constructed from three monolingual sentence-aligned paraphrase subcorpora from differing text genres, with word-level alignments provided by two human annotators. We parse each corpus sentence pair using the OpenCCG parser to yield a logical form (LF) as a semantic dependency graph with the gold-standard alignments projected onto the LF pair. Disjunctive LFs are then constructed by inspecting the graph structure of each LF in comparison with the other. Here, an alignment is represented simply as a pair $\langle n1, n2\rangle$ where $n1$ is a node in the first LF and $n2$ a node in the second LF. As Cohn et al.'s corpus contains some **block alignments**, there are cases where a single node is aligned to multiple nodes in the other sentence of the paraphrase.

A semantic dependency is represented as graph $\mathcal{G} = \langle N, E\rangle$, where $N = \mathsf{nodes}(\mathcal{G})$ is the set of nodes in $\mathcal{G}$ and $E = \mathsf{edges}(\mathcal{G})$ is the set of edges in $\mathcal{G}$. An edge e is a labeled dependency between nodes, with $\mathsf{source}(e)$ denoting the source node, $\mathsf{target}(e)$ the target node, and $\mathsf{label}(e)$ the relation e represents. For $n, n' \in \mathsf{nodes}(\mathcal{G})$ members of the set of nodes for some graph $\mathcal{G}$, $n' \in \mathsf{parents}(n)$ if and only if there is an edge $e \in \mathsf{edges}(\mathcal{G})$ with $n' = \mathsf{source}(e)$ and $n = \mathsf{target}(e)$. The set $\mathsf{ancestors}(n)$ models the transitive closure of the 'parent-of' relation: $a \in \mathsf{ancestors}(n)$ if and only if there is some $p \in \mathsf{parents}(n)$ such that either $a = p$ or $a \in \mathsf{ancestors}(p)$. Nodes in a graph additionally bear associated predicates and semantic features that are derived during the parsing process.

3.1 The Algorithm

As a preprocessing step, we first characterize the difference between two LFs as a set of edit operations via MAKEEDITS$(g1, g2, alignments)$, as detailed in Algorithm 1. An **insert** results when the second graph contains an unaligned subgraph. Similarly, an unaligned subgraph in the first LF is characterized by a **delete** operation. For both inserts and deletes, only the head of the inserted or deleted subgraph is represented as an edit in order to reflect the fact that these operations can encompass entire subgraphs. A **substitution** occurs when a subgraph in the first LF is aligned to one or more subgraphs in the second LF. The case where subgraphs are block aligned corresponds to a multi-word phrasal substitution (for example, the substitution of *Goldman* for *The US investment bank* in paraphrase (2), below). The DLF generation process is then driven by these edit operations.

DLFs are created for each sentence by DISJUNCTIVIZE$(g1, g2, alignments)$ and DISJUNCTIVIZE$(g2, g1, alignments)$, respectively, where $g1$ is the first sentence's LF and $g2$ the LF of the second (see Algorithm 2). The DLF construction process takes as inputs a pair of dependency graphs $\langle g1, g2\rangle$ and a set of word-level alignments from Cohn et al.'s (2008) paraphrase corpus projected onto the graphs. This process creates a DLF by merging or making optional material from the sec-

[3]To be precise, the HLDS logical forms are descriptions of semantic dependency graphs, which in turn can be interpreted model theoretically via translation to Discourse Representation Theory (Kamp and Reyle, 1993), as White (2006b) explains. A disjunctive logical form is thus a description of a set of semantic dependency graphs. (As the LFs derived using CCGbank grammars do not represent quantifier scope properly, it would be more accurate to call them quasi-LFs; as this issue does not appear to impact the realization or DLF creation algorithms, however, we have employed the simpler term.)

Algorithm 1 Preprocesses a pair of aligned LFs representing a paraphrase into edit operations.

procedure MAKEEDITS($g1, g2, alignments$)
  for all $i \in \{n \in \text{nodes}(g2) \mid \neg\exists x.\langle x, n\rangle \in alignments\}$ **do** ▷ inserts
    if $\neg\exists p.p \in \text{parents}(i) \wedge \neg\exists x.\langle x, p\rangle \in alignments$ **then**
      $\text{insert}(i)$
  for all $d \in \{n \in \text{nodes}(g1) \mid \neg\exists y.\langle n, y\rangle \in alignments\}$ **do** ▷ deletes
    if $\neg\exists p.p \in \text{parents}(d) \wedge \neg\exists y.\langle p, y\rangle \in alignments$ **then**
      $\text{delete}(d)$
  for all $s \in \text{nodes}(g1)$ **do** ▷ substitutions
    if $\exists y.\langle s, y\rangle \in alignments \wedge \neg\exists z.z \in \text{parents}(y) \wedge \langle s, z\rangle \in alignments$ **then**
      $\text{substitution}(s, y)$

Algorithm 2 Constructs a disjunctive LF from an aligned paraphrase.

procedure DISJUNCTIVIZE($g1, g2, alignments$)
  MAKEEDITS($g1, g2, alignments$)
  for all $i \in \{n \in \text{nodes}(g2) \mid \text{insert}(n)\}$ **do**
    for all $p \in \{e \in \text{edges}(g2) \mid i = \text{target}(e)\}$ **do**
      for all $\langle n1, n2\rangle \in \{\langle x, y\rangle \in alignments \mid y = \text{source}(p)\}$ **do**
        $\text{option}(n1, p)$
  for all $d \in \{n \in \text{nodes}(g1) \mid \text{delete}(n)\}$ **do**
    for all $p \in \{e \in \text{edges}(g1) \mid d = \text{target}(e)\}$ **do**
      $\text{option}(\text{source}(p), p)$
  for all $s \in \{n \in \text{nodes}(g1) \mid \exists y.\text{substitution}(n, y)\}$ **do**
    for all $p \in \text{parents}(s)$ **do**
      $\text{choice}(p, \{e \in \text{edges}(g2) \mid \text{substitution}(s, \text{target}(e)) \wedge \langle p, \text{source}(e)\rangle \in alignments\})$

ond LF into the first LF.

As Algorithm 2 describes, first the inserts (line 3) and deletes (line 7) are handled. In the case of inserts, for each node i in the second LF that is the head of an inserted subgraph, we find every $n2$ that is the source of an edge p whose target is i. The edge p is added as an option for each node $n1$ in the first LF that is aligned to $n2$. The process for deletes is similar, modulo direction reversal. We find every edge p whose target is d, where d is the head of an unaligned subgraph in the first sentence, and make p an option for the parent node source(p). With both inserts and deletes, the intuitive idea is that an unaligned subgraph should be treated as an optional dependency from its parent.

The following corpus sentence pair demonstrates the handling of inserts/deletes:

(1) a. Justices said that the constitution allows the government to administer drugs only in limited circumstances.

b. In a 6-3 ruling, the justices said such anti-psychotic drugs can be used only in limited circumstances.

In the DLF constructed for (1a), the node representing the word *drugs* has two alternate children that are not present in the first sentence itself (i.e., are inserted), *such* and *anti-psychotic*, both of which are in the modifier relation to *drugs*. This happens because *drugs* is aligned to the word *drugs* in (1b), which has the modifier child nodes. The second sentence also contains the insertion *In a 6-3 ruling*. This entire subgraph is represented as an optional modifier of *said*. Finally, the determiner *the* is inserted before *justices* in the second sentence. This determiner is also represented as an optional edge from *justices*. Figure 2 shows the portion of the DLF reflecting the optional modifier *In a 6-3 ruling* and optional determiner *the*.

For substitutions (line 10), we consider each subgraph-heading node s in the first LF that is substituted for some node y in the second LF that is also a subgraph head. Then for each parent p of s, the choices for p are contained in the set of edges whose source is aligned to p and whose target is a substitution for s. The intuition is that for each node p in the first LF with an aligned subgraph c, there is a disjunction between c and the child subgraphs of the

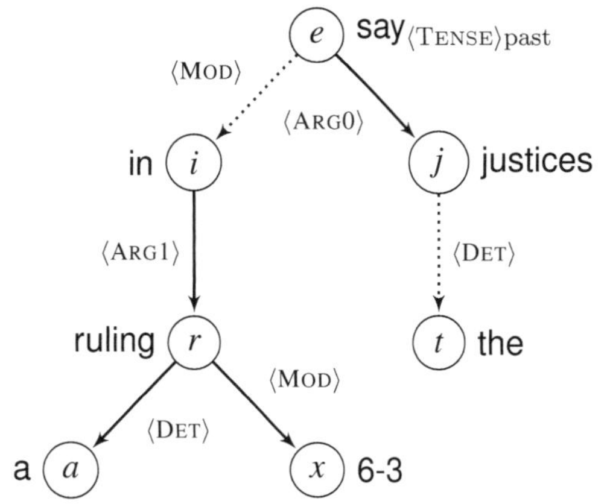

Figure 2: Disjunctive LF subgraph for the alternation *(In a 6-3 ruling)? (the)? justices said ...* in paraphrase (1). The dotted lines represent optional edges, and some semantic features are suppressed for readability.

node that p is aligned to in the second LF. For efficiency, in the special case of substitutions involving single nodes rather than entire subgraphs, only the semantic predicates are disjoined.[4]

To demonstrate, consider the following corpus sentence pair involving a phrasal substitution:

(2) a. The US investment bank said: we believe the long-term prospects for the energy sector in the UK remain attractive.

b. We believe the long-term prospects for the energy sector in the UK remain attractive, Goldman said.

In this paraphrase, the subtree *The US investment bank* in (2a) is aligned to the single word *Goldman* in (2b), but their predicates are obviously different. The constructed DLF contains a choice between *Goldman* and *The US investment bank* as the subject of *said*. Figure 3 illustrates the relevant subgraph of the DLF constructed from the *Goldman* paraphrase with a choice between subjects (⟨ARG0⟩). This disjunction arises because *said* in the first sentence is aligned to *said* in the second, and *The US investment bank* is the subject of *said* in the first while *Goldman* is its subject in the second. Note that, since the substitution is a phrasal (block-aligned) one, the constructed DLF forces a choice between *Goldman* and the entire subgraph headed by *bank*, not between

[4]We leave certain more complex cases, e.g. multiple nodes with aligned children, for future work.

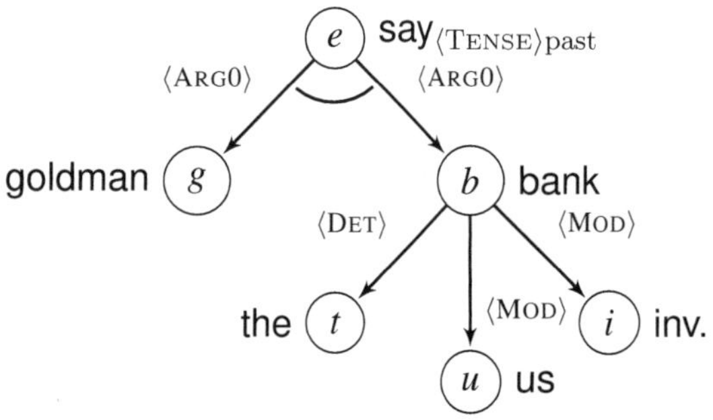

Figure 3: Disjunctive LF subgraph for the alternation (*Goldman* | *The US investment bank*) *said* ... in paraphrase (2). The arc represents the two choice edges for the ⟨ARG0⟩ relation from *say*. Certain semantic dependencies are omitted, and the word *investment* is abbreviated to save space.

Goldman and each of *bank*'s dependents (*the, US,* and *investment*).

4 Discussion and Future Work

With a broad coverage grammar, we have found that most of the realization alternatives in an n-best list tend to reuse the same lexical choices, with the differences mostly consisting of alternate word orders or use of function words or punctuation. Accordingly, in order to enhance the variety of word and phrase choices in the n-best lists, we have taken advantage of the API-level support for plugging in custom pruning strategies and developed a custom strategy that encourages lexical diversity. This strategy groups realizations that share the same open class stems into equivalence classes, where new equivalence classes are favored over new alternatives within the same equivalence class in filling up the n-best list.

Using this lexical diversity pruning strategy, an example of the paraphrases generated after DLF creation appears in Table 2. In the example, *the girl* and *brianna* are successfully alternated, as are *her mother's* and *the (bedroom)*. The example also includes a reasonable Heavy-NP shift, with *into the bedroom* appearing before the NP list. Without the lexical diversity pruning strategy, the phrase *her mother's* does not find its way into the n-best list. The paraphrases also include a mistaken change in tense from *had* to *has* and a mysterious inclusion of *including*. Interestingly though, these mistakes follow in the n-best list alternatives that are otherwise the same, suggesting that a final pruning of the list may make it possible to keep only generally good paraphrases. (Note that the appositive *33* in the second reference sentence also has been dropped, most likely since the pruning strategy does not include numbers in the set of content words at present.)

Although we have not yet formally evaluated the paraphrases, we can already characterize some recurring errors. Named entities are an issue since we have not incorporated a named entity recognizer; thus, the realizer is apt to generate *O. Charles Prince* instead of *Charles O. Prince*, for example. Worse, *medical examiner 's spokeswoman ellen borakove* is realized both correctly and as *medical examiner 's ellen spokeswoman borakove*. Naturally, there are also paraphrasing errors that stem from parser errors. Certainly with named entities, though perhaps also with parser errors, we plan to investigate whether we can take advantage of the word order in the reference sentence in order to reduce the number of mistakes. Here, we plan to investigate whether a feature measuring similarity in word order to the original can be balanced against the averaged perceptron model score in a way that allows new paraphrases to be generated while sticking to the original order in cases of uncertainty. Initial experiments with adding to the perceptron model score an n-gram precision score (approximating BLEU) with an appropriate weight indicate that realizations including the correct word order in names such as *Charles O. Prince* can be pushed to the top of the n-best list, though it remains to be verified that the weight for the similarity score can be adequately tuned with held-out data. Incorporating a measure of similarity to the original reference sentences into realization ranking is a form of what Madnani (2010) calls a **self-paraphrase bias**, though a different one than his method of adjusting the probability mass assigned to the original.

In future work, we plan to evaluate the generated paraphrases both intrinsically and extrinsically in combination with MT evaluation metrics. With the intrinsic evaluation, we expect to examine the impact of parser and alignment errors on the paraphrases, and the extent to which these can be mitigated by a self-paraphrase bias, along with the impact of the lexical diversity pruning strategy on the

Reference 1	lee said brianna had dragged food , toys and other things into the bedroom .
Realizations	lee said *the girl* had dragged food , toys and other things into the bedroom .
	lee said brianna had dragged food , toys and other things into the bedroom .
	lee said , the girl had dragged [into the bedroom] food , toys and other things .
	lee said the girl has dragged into the bedroom food , toys and other things .
	lee said , brianna had dragged into the bedroom food , toys and other things .
	lee said the girl had dragged food , toys and other things into *her mother 's* bedroom .
	lee said , the girl had dragged into her mother 's bedroom food , toys and other things .
	lee said brianna had dragged food , toys and other things into her mother 's bedroom .
	lee said the girl had dragged food , toys and other things into including the bedroom .
	lee said , brianna had dragged into her mother 's bedroom food , toys and other things .
Reference 2	lee , 33 , said the girl had dragged the food , toys and other things into her mother 's bedroom .
Realizations	lee said the girl had dragged [into *the* bedroom] the food , toys and other things .
	lee said , the girl had dragged into the bedroom the food , toys and other things .
	lee said the girl has dragged into the bedroom the food , toys and other things .
	lee said *brianna* had dragged the food , toys and other things into the bedroom .
	lee said , brianna had dragged into the bedroom the food , toys and other things .
	lee said the girl had dragged the food , toys and other things into her mother 's bedroom .
	lee said brianna had dragged into her mother 's bedroom the food , toys and other things .
	lee said , the girl had dragged into her mother 's bedroom the food , toys and other things .
	lee said brianna had dragged the food , toys and other things into her mother 's bedroom .
	lee said the girl had dragged the food , toys and other things into including the bedroom .

Table 2: Example n-best realizations starting from each reference sentence. Alternative phrasings from the other member of the pair are shown in italics the first time, and alternative phrase locations are shown in square brackets. Mistakes are underlined, and suppressed after the first occurrence in the list.

number of acceptable paraphrases in the n-best list.

With the extrinsic evaluation, we plan to investigate whether n-best paraphrase generation using the methods described here can be used to augment a set of reference translations in such a way as to increase the correlation of automatic metrics with human judgments. As Madnani observes, generated paraphrases of reference translations may be either untargeted or targeted to specific MT hypotheses. In the case of targeted paraphrases, the generated paraphrases then approximate the process by which automatic translations are evaluated using HTER (Snover et al., 2006), with a human in the loop, as the closest acceptable paraphrase of a reference sentence should correspond to the version of the MT hypothesis with minimal changes to make it acceptable. While in principle we might similarly acquire paraphrase rules using the pivot method, as in Madnani's approach, such rules would be quite noisy, as it is a difficult problem to characterize the contexts in which words or phrases can be acceptably substituted. Thus, our immediate focus will be on generating synthetic references with high precision, relying on grammatical alternations plus contextually acceptable alternatives present in multiple reference translations, given that metrics such as METEOR (Banerjee and Lavie, 2005) and TERp (Snover et al., 2010) can now employ paraphrase matching as part of their scoring, complementing what can be done with our methods. To the extent that we can maintain high precision in generating synthetic reference sentences, we may expect the correlations between automatic metric scores and human judgments to improve as the task of the metrics becomes simpler.

Acknowledgements

This work was supported in part by NSF grant number IIS-0812297. We are also grateful to Trevor Cohn for help with the paraphrase data.

References

Jason Baldridge and Geert-Jan Kruijff. 2002. Coupling CCG and Hybrid Logic Dependency Semantics. In *Proc. ACL-02*.

Jason Baldridge. 2002. *Lexically Specified Derivational*

Control in Combinatory Categorial Grammar. Ph.D. thesis, School of Informatics, University of Edinburgh.

Satanjeev Banerjee and Alon Lavie. 2005. METEOR: An Automatic Metric for MT Evaluation with Improved Correlation with Human Judgments. In *Proc. of the ACL-05 Workshop on Intrinsic and Extrinsic Evaluation Measures for Machine Translation and/or Summarization*.

Colin Bannard and Chris Callison-Burch. 2005. Paraphrasing with bilingual parallel corpora. In *Proc. ACL-05*, pages 597–604.

Regina Barzilay and Lillian Lee. 2003. Learning to paraphrase: An unsupervised approach using multiple-sequence alignment. In *Proc. of NAACL-HLT*.

Regina Barzilay and Kathleen McKeown. 2005. Sentence fusion for multidocument news summarization. *Computational Linguistics*, 31(3):297–327.

Stephen Boxwell and Michael White. 2008. Projecting Propbank roles onto the CCGbank. In *Proc. LREC-08*.

Stephen Clark and James R. Curran. 2007. Wide-Coverage Efficient Statistical Parsing with CCG and Log-Linear Models. *Computational Linguistics*, 33(4):493–552.

Trevor Cohn, Chris Callison-Burch, and Mirella Lapata. 2008. Constructing corpora for the development and evaluation of paraphrase systems. *Computational Linguistics*, 34(4):597–614.

M. Elhadad, J. Robin, and K. McKeown. 1997. Floating constraints in lexical choice. *Computational Linguistics*, 23(2):195–239.

Dominic Espinosa, Michael White, and Dennis Mehay. 2008. Hypertagging: Supertagging for surface realization with CCG. In *Proceedings of ACL-08: HLT*, pages 183–191, Columbus, Ohio, June. Association for Computational Linguistics.

Mary Ellen Foster and Michael White. 2007. Avoiding repetition in generated text. In *Proceedings of the 11th European Workshop on Natural Language Generation (ENLG 2007)*.

Claire Gardent and Eric Kow. 2005. Generating and selecting grammatical paraphrases. In *Proc. ENLG-05*.

Aria Haghighi, John Blitzer, John DeNero, and Dan Klein. 2009. Better word alignments with supervised ITG models. In *Proceedings of ACL*, pages 923–931, Suntec, Singapore, August. Association for Computational Linguistics.

Julia Hockenmaier and Mark Steedman. 2002. Generative models for statistical parsing with Combinatory Categorial Grammar. In *Proc. ACL-02*.

Julia Hockenmaier and Mark Steedman. 2007. CCGbank: A Corpus of CCG Derivations and Dependency Structures Extracted from the Penn Treebank. *Computational Linguistics*, 33(3):355–396.

Deirdre Hogan, Jennifer Foster, Joachim Wagner, and Josef van Genabith. 2008. Parser-based retraining for domain adaptation of probabilistic generators. In *Proc. INLG-08*.

Lidija Iordanskaja, Richard Kittredge, and Alain Polgúere. 1991. Lexical selection and paraphrase in a meaning-text generation model. In Cécile L. Paris, William R. Swartout, and William C. Mann, editors, *Natural Language Generation in Artificial Intelligence and Computational Linguistics*, pages 293–312. Kluwer.

Hans Kamp and Uwe Reyle. 1993. *From Discourse to Logic*. Kluwer.

David Kauchak and Regina Barzilay. 2006. Paraphrasing for automatic evaluation. In *Proceedings of HLT-NAACL*.

Martin Kay. 1996. Chart generation. In *Proc. ACL-96*.

Irene Langkilde and Kevin Knight. 1998. The practical value of n-grams in generation. In *Proc. INLG-98*.

Irene Langkilde-Geary. 2002. An empirical verification of coverage and correctness for a general-purpose sentence generator. In *Proc. INLG-02*.

Bill MacCartney, Michel Galley, and Christopher D. Manning. 2008. A phrase-based alignment model for natural language inference. In *Proceedings of the 2008 Conference on Empirical Methods in Natural Language Processing*, pages 802–811, Honolulu, Hawaii, October. Association for Computational Linguistics.

Nitin Madnani. 2010. *The Circle of Meaning: From Translation to Paraphrasing and Back*. Ph.D. thesis, Department of Computer Science, University of Maryland College Park.

Crystal Nakatsu and Michael White. 2006. Learning to say it well: Reranking realizations by predicted synthesis quality. In *Proc. COLING-ACL-06*.

Franz Josef Och and Hermann Ney. 2003. A systematic comparison of various statistical alignment models. *Computational Linguistics*, 1(29):19–52.

Martha Palmer, Daniel Gildea, and Paul Kingsbury. 2005. The proposition bank: An annotated corpus of semantic roles. *Computational Linguistics*, 31(1):71–106.

Bo Pang, Kevin Knight, and Daniel Marcu. 2003. Syntax-based alignment of multiple translations: Extracting paraphrases and generating new sentences. In *Proc. HLT/NAACL*.

Kishore Papineni, Salim Roukos, Todd Ward, and Wei-Jing Zhu. 2002. BLEU: a method for automatic evaluation of machine translation. In *Proc. ACL-02*.

Brian Roark, Murat Saraclar, Michael Collins, and Mark Johnson. 2004. Discriminative language modeling with conditional random fields and the perceptron algorithm. In *Proc. ACL-04*.

Hadar Shemtov. 1997. *Ambiguity Management in Natural Language Generation*. Ph.D. thesis, Stanford University.

Matthew Snover, Bonnie Dorr, Richard Schwartz, Linnea Micciulla, and John Makhoul. 2006. A study of translation edit rate with targeted human annotation. In *Proc. of the Association for Machine Translation in the Americas (AMTA-06)*.

Matthew Snover, Nitin Madnani, Bonnie Dorr, and Richard Schwartz. 2010. TER-plus: Paraphrase, semantic, and alignment enhancements to translation edit rate. *Machine Translation*, 23:117–127.

M. Stede. 1999. *Lexical Semantics and Knowledge Representation in Multilingual Text Generation*. Kluwer Academic Publishers.

Mark Steedman. 2000. *The Syntactic Process*. MIT Press.

Erik Velldal, Stephan Oepen, and Dan Flickinger. 2004. Paraphrasing treebanks for stochastic realization ranking. In *Proceedings of the 3rd Workshop on Treebanks and Linguistic Theories*.

Michael White and Rajakrishnan Rajkumar. 2009. Perceptron reranking for CCG realization. In *Proceedings of the 2009 Conference on Empirical Methods in Natural Language Processing*, pages 410–419, Singapore, August. Association for Computational Linguistics.

Michael White. 2004. Reining in CCG Chart Realization. In *Proc. INLG-04*.

Michael White. 2006a. CCG chart realization from disjunctive logical forms. In *Proc. INLG-06*.

Michael White. 2006b. Efficient Realization of Coordinate Structures in Combinatory Categorial Grammar. *Research on Language & Computation*, 4(1):39–75.

Shiqi Zhao, Xiang Lan, Ting Liu, and Sheng Li. 2009. Application-driven statistical paraphrase generation. In *Proceedings of the Joint Conference of the 47th Annual Meeting of the ACL and the 4th International Joint Conference on Natural Language Processing of the AFNLP*, pages 834–842, Suntec, Singapore, August. Association for Computational Linguistics.

Paraphrastic Sentence Compression with a Character-based Metric: Tightening without Deletion

Courtney Napoles[1] and **Chris Callison-Burch**[1] and **Juri Ganitkevitch**[1] and **Benjamin Van Durme**[1,2]
[1]Department of Computer Science
[2]Human Language Technology Center of Excellence
Johns Hopkins University

Abstract

We present a substitution-only approach to sentence compression which "tightens" a sentence by reducing its character length. Replacing phrases with shorter paraphrases yields paraphrastic compressions as short as 60% of the original length. In support of this task, we introduce a novel technique for re-ranking paraphrases extracted from bilingual corpora. At high compression rates[1] paraphrastic compressions outperform a state-of-the-art deletion model in an oracle experiment. For further compression, deleting from oracle paraphrastic compressions preserves more meaning than deletion alone. In either setting, paraphrastic compression shows promise for surpassing deletion-only methods.

1 Introduction

Sentence compression is the process of shortening a sentence while preserving the most important information. Because it was developed in support of extractive summarization (Knight and Marcu, 2000), much of the previous work considers deletion-based models, which extract a subset of words from a long sentence to create a shorter sentence such that meaning and grammar are maximally preserved. This framework imposes strict constraints on the task and does not accurately model human-written compressions, which tend to be abstractive rather than extractive (Marsi et al., 2010). This is one sense in which paraphrastic compression can improve existing compression methodologies.

[1]Compression rate is defined as the compression length over original length, so lower values indicate shorter sentences.

We distinguish two non-identical notions of sentence compression: making a sentence substantially shorter versus "tightening" a sentence by removing unnecessary verbiage. We propose a method to tighten sentences with just substitution and no deletion operations. Using paraphrases extracted from bilingual text and re-ranked on monolingual data, our system selects the set of paraphrases that minimizes the character length of a sentence.

While not currently the standard, character-based lengths have been considered before in compression, and we believe that it is relevant for current and future applications. Character lengths have been used for document summarization (DUC 2004, Over and Yen (2004)), summarizing for mobile devices (Corston-Oliver, 2001), and subtitling (Glickman et al., 2006). Although in the past strict word limits have been imposed for various documents, information transmitted electronically is often limited by the number of bytes, which directly relates to the number of characters. Mobile devices, SMS messages, and microblogging sites such as Twitter are increasingly important for quickly spreading information. In this context, it is important to consider character-based constraints.

We examine whether paraphrastic compression allows more information to be conveyed in the same number of characters as deletion-only compressions. For example, the length constraint of Twitter posts or *tweets* is 140 characters, and many article lead sentences exceed this limit. A paraphrase substitution oracle compresses the sentence in the table below to 76% of its original length (162 to 123 characters; the first is the original). The compressed tweet is 140 characters, including spaces 17-character shortened link to the original article.[2]

Congressional leaders reached a last-gasp agreement Friday to avert a shutdown of the federal government, after days of haggling and tense hours of brinksmanship.
Congress made a final agreement Fri. to avoid government shutdown, after days of haggling and tense hours of brinkmanship. on.wsj.com/h8N7n1

In contrast, using deletion to compress to the same length may not be as expressive:

Congressional leaders reached agreement Friday to avert a shutdown of federal government, after haggling and tense hours. on.wsj.com/h8N7n1

This work presents a model that makes paraphrase choices to minimize the *character* length of a sentence. An oracle paraphrase-substitution experiment shows that human judges rate paraphrastic compressions higher than deletion-based compressions. To achieve further compression, we shortened the oracle compressions using a deletion model to yield compressions 80% of the original sentence length and compared these to compressions generated using just deletions. Manual evaluation found that the oracle-then-deletion compressions to preserve more meaning than deletion-only compressions at uniform compression rates.

2 Related work

Most of the previous research on sentence compression focuses on deletion using syntactic information, (e.g., Galley and McKeown (2007), Knight and Marcu (2002), Nomoto (2009), Galanis and Androutsopoulos (2010), Filippova and Strube (2008), McDonald (2006), Yamangil and Shieber (2010), Cohn and Lapata (2008), Cohn and Lapata (2009), Turner and Charniak (2005)). Woodsend et al. (2010) incorporate paraphrase rules into a deletion model. Previous work in subtitling has made one-word substitutions to decrease character length at high compression rates (Glickman et al., 2006). More recent approaches in steganography have used paraphrase substitution to encode information in text but focus on grammaticality, not meaning preservation (Chang and Clark, 2010). Zhao et al. (2009) applied an adaptable paraphrasing pipeline to sentence compression, optimizing for F-measure over a manually annotated set of gold standard paraphrases.

Sentence compression has been considered before in contexts outside of summarization, such as headline, title, and subtitle generation (Dorr et al., 2003; Vandeghinste and Pan, 2004; Marsi et al., 2009). Corston-Oliver (2001) deleted characters from words to shorten the character length of sentences. To our knowledge character-based compression has not been examined before with the surging popularity and utility of Twitter.

3 Sentence Tightening

The distinction between tightening and compression can be illustrated by considering how much space needs to be preserved. In the case of microblogging, often a sentence has just a few too many characters and needs to be "tightened". On the other hand, if a sentence is much longer than a desired length, more drastic compression is necessary. The first subtask is relevant in any context with strict word or character limits. Some sentences may not be compressible beyond a certain limit. For example, we found that near 10% of the compressions generated by Clarke and Lapata (2008) were identical to the original sentence. In situations where the sentence *must* meet a minimum length, tightening can be used to meet these requirements.

Multi-reference translations provide an instance of the natural length variation of human-generated sentences. These translations represent different ways to express the foreign same sentence, so there should be no meaning lost between the different reference translations. The character-based length of different translations of a given sentence varies on average by 80% when compared to the shortest sentence in a set.[3] This provides evidence that sentences can be tightened to some extent without losing any meaning.

Through the lens of sentence tightening, we consider whether paraphrase substitutions alone can yield compressions competitive with a deletion at the same length. A character-based compression rate is crucial in this framework, as two compres-

[2]Taken from the main page of http://wsj.com, April 9, 2011.

[3]This value will vary by collection and with the number of references: for example, the NIST05 Arabic reference set has a mean compression rate of 0.92 with 4 references per set.

sions having the same *character*-based compression rate may have different *word*-based compression rates. The advantage of a character-based substitution model is in choosing shorter words when possible, freeing space for more content words. Going by word length alone would exclude the many paraphrases with fewer characters than the original phrase and the same number of words (or more).

3.1 Paraphrase Acquisition

To generate paraphrases for use in our experiments, we took the approach described by Bannard and Callison-Burch (2005), which extracts paraphrases from bilingual parallel corpora. Figure 1 illustrates the process. A phrase to be paraphrased, like *thrown into jail*, is found in a German-English parallel corpus. The corresponding foreign phrase (*festgenommen*) is identified using word alignment and phrase extraction techniques from phrase-based statistical machine translation (Koehn et al., 2003). Other occurrences of the foreign phrase in the parallel corpus may align to another English phrase like *jailed*. Following Bannard and Callison-Burch, we treated any English phrases that share a common foreign phrase as potential paraphrases of each other.

As the original phrase occurs several times and aligns with many different foreign phrases, each of these may align to a variety of other English paraphrases. Thus, *thrown into jail* not only paraphrases as *jailed*, but also as *arrested*, *detained*, *imprisoned*, *incarcerated*, *locked up*, *taken into custody*, and *thrown into prison* . Moreover, because the method relies on noisy and potentially inaccurate word alignments, it is prone to generate many bad paraphrases, such as *maltreated*, *thrown*, *cases*, *custody*, *arrest*, *owners*, and *protection*.

To rank candidates, Bannard and Callison-Burch defined the paraphrase probability $p(e_2|e_1)$ based on the translation model probabilities $p(e|f)$ and $p(f|e)$ from statistical machine translation. Following Callison-Burch (2008), we refine selection by requiring both the original phrase and paraphrase to be of the same syntactic type, which leads to more grammatical paraphrases.

Although many excellent paraphrases are extracted from parallel corpora, many others are unsuitable and the translation score does not always accurately distinguish the two. Therefore, we re-

Paraphrase	Monlingual	Bilingual
study in detail	1.00	0.70
scrutinise	0.94	0.08
consider	0.90	0.20
keep	0.83	0.03
learn	0.57	0.10
study	0.42	0.07
studied	0.28	0.01
studying it in detail	0.16	0.05
undertook	0.06	0.06

Table 1: Candidate paraphrases for *study in detail* with corresponding approximate cosine similarity (Monolingual) and translation model (Bilingual) scores.

ranked our candidates based on monolingual distributional similarity, employing the method described by Van Durme and Lall (2010) to derive approximate cosine similarity scores over feature counts using single token, independent left and right contexts. Features were computed from the web-scale n-gram collection of Lin et al. (2010). As 5-grams are the highest order of n-gram in this collection, the allowable set of paraphrases have at most four words (which allows at least one word of context).

To our knowledge this is the first time such techniques have been used in combination in order to derive higher quality paraphrase candidates. See Table 1 for an example.

The monolingual-filtering technique we describe is by no means limited to paraphrases extracted from bilingual corpora. It could be applied to other data-driven paraphrasing techniques (see Madnani and Dorr (2010) for a survey). Although it is particularly well suited to the bilingual extracted corpora, since the information that it adds is orthogonal to that model, it would presumably add less to paraphrasing techniques that already take advantage of monolingual distributional similarity (Pereira et al., 1993; Lin and Pantel, 2001; Barzilay and Lee, 2003).

In order to evaluate the paraphrase candidates and scoring techniques, we randomly selected 1,000 paraphrase sets where the source phrase was present in the corpus described in Clarke and Lapata (2008). For each phrase and set of candidate paraphrases, we extracted all of the contexts from the corpus in which the source phrase appeared. Human judges were presented each sentence with the original phrase and the same sentences with each paraphrase candidate

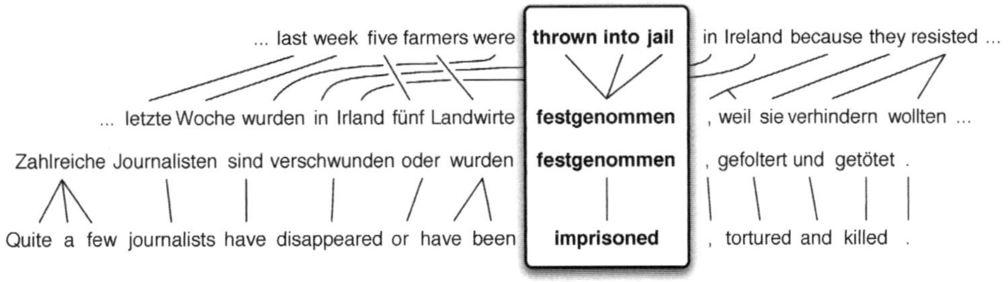

Figure 1: Using a bilingual parallel corpus to extract paraphrases.

substituted in. Each paraphrase substitution was graded based on the extent to which it preserved the meaning and affected the grammaticality of the sentence. While both the bilingual translation score and monolingual cosine similarity positively correlated with human judgments, the monolingual score proved a stronger predictor of quality in both dimensions. Using Kendall's tau correlation coefficient, the agreement between the ranking imposed by the monolingual score and human ratings surpassed that of the original ranking as derived during the bilingual extraction, for both meaning and grammar.[4] In our substitution framework, we ignore the translation probabilities and use only the approximate cosine similarity in the paraphrase decision task.

4 Framework for Sentence Tightening

Our sentence tightening approach uses a dynamic programming strategy to find the combination of non-overlapping paraphrases that minimizes a sentence's character length. The threshold of the monolingual score for paraphrases can be varied to widen or narrow the search space, which may be further increased by considering any lexical paraphrases not subject to syntactic constraints. Sentences with a compression rate as low as 0.6 can be generated without thresholding the paraphrase scores. Because the system can generate multiple paraphrased sentences of equal length, we apply two layers of filtering to generate a single output. First we calculate a word-overlap score between the original and candidate sentences to favor compressions similar to the original sentence; then, from among the sentences with the highest word overlap, we select the compression with the best language model score.

Higher paraphrase thresholds guarantee more appropriate paraphrases but yield longer compressions. Using a cosine-similarity threshold of 0.95, the average compression rate is 0.968, which is considerably longer than the compressions using no threshold (0.60). In these experiments we did not syntactically constrain paraphrases. However, we believe that our monolingual refining of paraphrase sets improves paraphrase selection and is a reasonable alternative to using syntactic constraints.

In case judges favor compressions that have high word overlap with the original sentence, we compressed the longest sentence from each set of reference translations (Huang et al., 2002) and randomly chose a sentence from the set of reference translations to use as the standard for comparison. Paraphrastic compressions were generated at cosine-similarity thresholds ranging from 0.60 to 0.95. We implemented a state-of-the-art deletion model (Clarke and Lapata, 2008) to generate deletion-only compressions. We fixed the compression length to ± 5 characters of the length of each paraphrastic compression, in order to isolate the compression quality from the effect of compression rate (Napoles et al., 2011). Manual evaluation used Amazon's Mechanical Turk with three-way redundancy and positive and negative controls to filter bad workers. Meaning and grammar judgments were collected using two 5-point scales (5 being the highest score).

5 Evaluation

The initial results of our substitution system show room for improvement in future work (Table 2). We believe this is due to erroneous paraphrase substi-

[4]For meaning and grammar respectively, $\tau = 0.28$ and 0.31 for monolingual scores and 0.19 and 0.15 for bilingual scores.

System	Grammar	Meaning	CompR	Cos.
Substitution	3.8	3.7	0.97	0.95
Deletion	4.1	4.0	0.97	-
Substitution	3.4	3.2	0.89	0.85
Deletion	4.0	3.8	0.89	-
Substitution	3.1	3.0	0.85	0.75
Deletion	3.9	3.7	0.85	-
Substitution	2.9	2.9	0.82	0.65
Deletion	3.8	3.5	0.82	-

Table 2: Mean ratings of compressions using just deletion or substitution at different paraphrase thresholds (Cos.). Deletion performed better in all settings.

tutions, since phrases with the same syntactic category and distributional similarity are not necessarily semantically identical. Illustrative examples include *WTO* for *United Nations* and *east* or *west* for *south*. Because the quality of the multi-reference translations is not uniformly high, for the following experiment we used a dataset of English newspaper articles.

To control against these errors and test the viability of a substitution-only approach, we generated all possible paraphrase substitutions above a threshold of 0.80 within a set of 20 randomly chosen sentences from the written corpus of Clarke and Lapata (2008). We solicited humans to make a ternary decision of whether a paraphrase was acceptable in the context (*good*, *bad*, or *not sure*). We applied our model to generate compressions using only paraphrase substitutions on which all three annotators agreed that the paraphrase was *good*. The oracle generated compressions with an average compression rate of 0.90.

On the same set of original sentences, we used the deletion model to generate compressions constrained to ±5 characters of the length of the oracle compression. Next, we examined whether applying the deletion model to paraphrastic compressions would improve compression quality. In manual evaluation along the dimensions of grammar and meaning, both the oracle compressions and oracle-plus-deletion compressions outperformed the deletion-only compressions at uniform lengths (Table 3)[5]. These results suggest that improvements in paraphrase acquisition will make our system competitive with deletion-only models.

[5]Paraphrastic compressions were rated significantly higher for meaning, $p < 0.05$

Model	Grammar	Meaning	CompR
Oracle	4.1	4.3	0.90
Deletion	4.0	4.1	0.90
Gold	4.3	3.8	0.75
Oracle+deletion	3.4	3.7	0.80
Deletion	3.2	3.4	0.80

Table 3: Mean ratings of compressions generated by a substitution oracle, deletion only, deletion on the oracle compression, and the gold standard. Being able to choose the best paraphrases would enable our substitution model to outperform the deletion model.

6 Conclusion

This work shows promise for the use of only substitution in the task of sentence tightening. There are myriad possible extensions and improvements to this method, most notably richer features beyond paraphrase length. We do not currently use syntactic information in our paraphrastic compression model because it places limits on the number of paraphrases available for a sentence and thereby limits the possible compression rate. The current method for paraphrase extraction does not include certain types of rewriting, such as passivization, and should be extended to incorporate even more shortening paraphrases. Future work can directly apply these methods to Twitter and extract additional paraphrases and abbreviations from Twitter and/or SMS data. Our substitution approach can be improved by applying more sophisticated techniques to choosing the best candidate compression, or by framing it as an optimization problem over more than just minimal length. Overall, we find these results to be encouraging for the possibility of sentence compression without deletion.

Acknowledgments

We are grateful to John Carroll for helping us obtain the RASP parser. This research was partially funded by the JHU Human Language Technology Center of Excellence. This research was funded in part by the NSF under grant IIS-0713448. The views and findings are the authors' alone.

References

Colin Bannard and Chris Callison-Burch. 2005. Paraphrasing with bilingual parallel corpora. In *Proceedings of ACL*.

Regina Barzilay and Lillian Lee. 2003. Learning to paraphrase: An unsupervised approach using multiple-sequence alignment. In *Proceedings of HLT/NAACL*.

Chris Callison-Burch. 2008. Syntactic constraints on paraphrases extracted from parallel corpora. In *Proceedings of EMNLP*.

Ching-Yun Chang and Stephen Clark. 2010. Linguistic steganography using automatically generated paraphrases. In *Human Language Technologies: The 2010 Annual Conference of the North American Chapter of the Association for Computational Linguistics*, pages 591–599. Association for Computational Linguistics.

James Clarke and Mirella Lapata. 2008. Global inference for sentence compression: An integer linear programming approach. *Journal of Artificial Intelligence Research*, 31:399–429.

Trevor Cohn and Mirella Lapata. 2008. Sentence compression beyond word deletion. In *Proceedings of COLING*.

Trevor Cohn and Mirella Lapata. 2009. Sentence compression as tree transduction. *Journal of Artificial Intelligence Research*, 34:637–674.

Simon Corston-Oliver. 2001. Text compaction for display on very small screens. In *Proceedings of the NAACL Workshop on Automatic Summarization*.

Bonnie Dorr, David Zajic, and Richard Schwartz. 2003. Hedge trimmer: A parse-and-trim approach to headline generation. In *Proceedings of the HLT-NAACL Workshop on Text summarization Workshop*.

Katja Filippova and Michael Strube. 2008. Dependency tree based sentence compression. In *Proceedings of the Fifth International Natural Language Generation Conference*. Association for Computational Linguistics.

Dimitrios Galanis and Ion Androutsopoulos. 2010. An extractive supervised two-stage method for sentence compression. In *Proceedings of NAACL*.

Michel Galley and Kathleen R. McKeown. 2007. Lexicalized Markov grammars for sentence compression. *the Proceedings of NAACL/HLT*.

Oren Glickman, Ido Dagan, Mikaela Keller, Samy Bengio, and Walter Daelemans. 2006. Investigating lexical substitution scoring for subtitle generation. In *Proceedings of the Tenth Conference on Computational Natural Language Learning*, pages 45–52. Association for Computational Linguistics.

Shudong Huang, David Graff, and George Doddington. 2002. Multiple-Translation Chinese Corpus. Linguistic Data Consortium.

Kevin Knight and Daniel Marcu. 2000. Statistics-based summarization – Step one: Sentence compression. In *Proceedings of AAAI*.

Kevin Knight and Daniel Marcu. 2002. Summarization beyond sentence extraction: A probabilistic approach to sentence compression. *Artificial Intelligence*, 139:91–107.

Philipp Koehn, Franz Josef Och, and Daniel Marcu. 2003. Statistical phrase-based translation. In *Proceedings of HLT/NAACL*.

Dekang Lin and Patrick Pantel. 2001. Discovery of inference rules from text. *Natural Language Engineering*, 7(3):343–360.

Dekang Lin, Kenneth Church, Heng Ji, Satoshi Sekine, David Yarowsky, Shane Bergsma, Kailash Patil, Emily Pitler, Rachel Lathbury, Vikram Rao, Kapil Dalwani, and Sushant Narsale. 2010. New Tools for Web-Scale N-grams. In *Proceedings of LREC*.

Nitin Madnani and Bonnie Dorr. 2010. Generating phrasal and sentential paraphrases: A survey of data-driven methods. *Computational Linguistics*, 36(3):341–388.

Erwin Marsi, Emiel Krahmer, Iris Hendrickx, and Walter Daelemans. 2009. Is sentence compression an NLG task? In *Proceedings of the 12th European Workshop on Natural Language Generation*.

Erwin Marsi, Emiel Krahmer, Iris Hendrickx, and Walter Daelemans. 2010. On the limits of sentence compression by deletion. *Empirical Methods in Natural Language Generation*, pages 45–66.

Ryan McDonald. 2006. Discriminative sentence compression with soft syntactic constraints. In *In Proceedings of EACL*.

Courtney Napoles, Benjamin Van Durme, and Chris Callison-Burch. 2011. Evaluating sentence compression: Pitfalls and suggested remedies. In *Proceedings of ACL, Workshop on Monolingual Text-To-Text Generation*.

Tadashi Nomoto. 2009. A comparison of model free versus model intensive approaches to sentence compression. In *Proceedings of EMNLP*.

Paul Over and James Yen. 2004. An introduction to DUC 2004: Intrinsic evaluation of generic news text summarization systems. In *Proceedings of DUC 2004 Document Understanding Workshop, Boston*.

Fernando Pereira, Naftali Tishby, and Lillian Lee. 1993. Distributional clustering of English words. In *ACL-93*.

Jenine Turner and Eugene Charniak. 2005. Supervised and unsupervised learning for sentence compression. In *Proceedings of ACL*.

Benjamin Van Durme and Ashwin Lall. 2010. Online generation of locality sensitive hash signatures. In *Proceedings of ACL, Short Papers*.

Vincent Vandeghinste and Yi Pan. 2004. Sentence compression for automated subtitling: A hybrid approach. In *Proceedings of the ACL workshop on Text Summarization*.

Kristian Woodsend, Yansong Feng, and Mirella Lapata. 2010. Generation with quasi-synchronous grammar. In *Proceedings of EMNLP*.

Elif Yamangil and Stuart M. Shieber. 2010. Bayesian synchronous tree-substitution grammar induction and its application to sentence compression. In *Proceedings of ACL*.

Shiqi Zhao, Xiang Lan, Ting Liu, and Sheng Li. 2009. Application-driven statistical paraphrase generation.

Evaluating sentence compression: Pitfalls and suggested remedies

Courtney Napoles[1] and **Benjamin Van Durme**[1,2] and **Chris Callison-Burch**[1]
[1]Department of Computer Science
[2]Human Language Technology Center of Excellence
Johns Hopkins University

Abstract

This work surveys existing evaluation methodologies for the task of sentence compression, identifies their shortcomings, and proposes alternatives. In particular, we examine the problems of evaluating paraphrastic compression and comparing the output of different models. We demonstrate that compression rate is a strong predictor of compression *quality* and that perceived improvement over other models is often a side effect of producing longer output.

1 Introduction

Sentence compression is the natural language generation (NLG) task of automatically shortening sentences. Because good compressions should be grammatical and retain important meaning, they must be evaluated along these two dimensions. Evaluation is a difficult problem for NLG, and many of the problems identified in this work are relevant for other generation tasks. Shared tasks are popular in many areas as a way to compare system performance in an unbiased manner. Unlike other tasks, such as machine translation, there is no shared-task evaluation for compression, even though some compression systems are indirectly evaluated as a part of DUC. The benefits of shared-task evaluation have been discussed before (e.g., Belz and Kilgarriff (2006) and Reiter and Belz (2006)), and they include comparing systems fairly under the same conditions.

One difficulty in evaluating compression systems fairly is that an unbiased automatic metric is hard to define. Automatic evaluation relies on a comparison to a single gold standard at a predetermined length, which greatly limits the types of compressions that can be fairly judged. As we will discuss in Section 2.1.1, automatic evaluation assumes that deletions are independent, considers only a single gold standard, and cannot handle compressions with paraphrasing. Like for most areas in NLG, human evaluation is preferable. However, as we discuss in Section 2.2, there are some subtleties to appropriate experiment design, which can give misleading results if not handled properly.

This work identifies the shortcomings of widely practiced evaluation methodologies and proposes alternatives. We report on the effect of compression rate on perceived quality and suggest ways to control for this dependency when evaluating across different systems. In this work we:

- highlight the importance of comparing systems with similar compression rates,
- argue that comparisons in many previous publications are invalid,
- provide suggestions for unbiased evaluation.

While many may find this discussion intuitive, these points are not addressed in much of the existing research, and therefore it is crucial to enumerate them in order to improve the scientific validity of the task.

2 Current Practices

Because it was developed in support of extractive summarization (Knight and Marcu, 2000), compression has mostly been framed as a deletion task (e.g., McDonald (2006), Galanis and Androutsopoulos (2010), Clarke and Lapata (2008), and Galley

Words	Sentence
31	*Kaczynski faces charges contained in a 10-count federal indictment naming him as the person responsible for transporting bombs and bomb parts from Montana to California and mailing them to victims .*
17	Kaczynski faces charges naming him responsible for transporting bombs to California and mailing them to victims .
18	Kaczynski faces charges naming him responsible for transporting bombs and bomb parts and mailing them to victims .
18	Kaczynski faces a 10-count federal indictment for transporting bombs and bomb parts and mailing them to victims .

Table 1: Three acceptable compressions of a sentence created by different annotators (the first is the original).

and McKeown (2007)). In this context, a compression is an extracted subset of words from a long sentence. There are limited compression corpora because, even when an aligned corpus exists, the number of extractive sentence pairs will be few and therefore gold-standard compressions must be manually annotated. The most popular corpora are the Ziff-Davis corpus (Knight and Marcu, 2000), which contains a small set of 1067 extracted sentences from article/abstract pairs, and the manually annotated Clarke and Lapata (2008) corpus, consisting of nearly 3000 sentences from news articles and broadcast news transcripts. These corpora contain one gold standard for each sentence.

2.1 Automatic Techniques

One of the most widely used automatic metrics is the F1 measure over grammatical relations of the gold-standard compressions (Riezler et al., 2003). This metric correlates significantly with human judgments and is better than Simple String Accuracy (Bangalore et al., 2000) for judging compression quality (Clarke and Lapata, 2006). F1 has also been used over unigrams (Martins and Smith, 2009) and bigrams (Unno et al., 2006). Unno et al. (2006) compared the F1 measures to BLEU scores (using the gold standard as a single reference) over varying compression rates, and found that BLEU behaves similarly to both F1 measures. A syntactic approach considers the alignment over parse trees (Jing, 2000), and a similar technique has been used with dependency trees to evaluate the quality of sentence fusions (Marsi and Krahmer, 2005).

The only metric that has been shown to correlate with human judgments is F1 (Clarke and Lapata, 2006), but even this is not entirely reliable. F1 over grammatical relations also depends on parser accuracy and the type of dependency relations used.[1]

2.1.1 Pitfalls of Automatic Evaluation

Automatic evaluation operates under three often incorrect assumptions:

Deletions are independent. The dependency structure of a sentence may be unaltered when dependent words are not deleted as a unit. Examples of words that should be treated as a single unit include negations and negative polarity items or certain multi-word phrases (such as deleting *Latin* and leaving *America*). F1 treats all deletions equally, when in fact errors of this type may dramatically alter the meaning or the grammaticality of a sentence and should be penalized more than less serious errors, such as deleting an article.

The gold standard is the single best compression. Automatic evaluation considers a single gold-standard compression. This ignores the possibility of different length compressions and equally good compressions of the same length, where multiple non-overlapping deletions are acceptable. For an example, see Table 1.

Having multiple gold standards would provide references at different compression lengths and reflect different deletion choices (see Section 3). Since no large corpus with multiple gold standards exists to our knowledge, systems could instead report the quality of compressions at several different compression rates, as Nomoto (2008) did. Alternatively, systems could evaluate compressions that are of a similar length as the gold standard compression, to fix a length for the purpose of evaluation. Output length is controlled for evaluation in some other areas, notably DUC.

Systems compress by deletion and not substitution. More recent approaches to compression introduce reordering and paraphrase operations (e.g.,

[1]For example, the RASP parser uses 16 grammatical dependencies (Briscoe, 2006) while there are over 50 Stanford Dependencies (de Marneffe and Manning, 2008).

Cohn and Lapata (2008), Woodsend et al. (2010), and Napoles et al. (2011)). For paraphrastic compressions, manual evaluation alone reliably determines the compression quality. Because automatic evaluation metrics compare shortened sentences to extractive gold standards, they cannot be applied to paraphrastic compression.

To apply automatic techniques to substitution-based compression, one would need a gold-standard set of paraphrastic compressions. These are rare. Cohn and Lapata (2008) created an abstractive corpus, which contains word reordering and paraphrasing in addition to deletion. Unfortunately, this corpus is small (575 sentences) and only includes one possible compression for each sentence.

Other alternatives include deriving such corpora from existing corpora of multi-reference translations. The longest reference translation can be paired with the shortest reference to represent a long sentence and corresponding paraphrased gold-standard compression.

Similar to machine translation or summarization, automatic translation of paraphrastic compressions would require *multiple references* to capture allowable variation, since there are often many equally valid ways of compressing an input. ROUGE or BLEU could be applied to a set of multiple-reference compressions, although BLEU is not without its own shortcomings (Callison-Burch et al., 2006). One benefit of both ROUGE and BLEU is that they are based on n-gram recall and precision (respectively) instead of word-error rate, so reordering and word substitutions can be evaluated. Dorr et al. (2003) used BLEU for evaluation in the context of headline generation, which uses rewording and is related to sentence compression. Alternatively, manual evalation can be adapted from other NLG domains, such as the techniques described in the following section.

2.2 Manual Evaluation

In order to determine semantic and syntactic suitability, manual evaluation is preferable over automatic techniques whenever possible. The most widely practiced manual evaluation methodology was first used by Knight and Marcu (2002). Judges grade each compressed sentence against the original and make two separate decisions: how grammatical is the compression and how much of the meaning from the original sentence is preserved. Decisions are rated along a 5-point scale (LDC, 2005).

Most compression systems consider sentences out of context (a few exceptions exist, e.g., Daumé III and Marcu (2002), Martins and Smith (2009), and Lin (2003)). Contextual cues and discourse structure may not be a factor to consider if the sentences are generated for use out of context. An example of a context-aware approach considered the summaries formed by shortened sentences and evaluated the compression systems based on how well people could answer questions about the original document from the summaries (Clarke and Lapata, 2007). This technique has been used before for evaluating summarization and text comprehension (Mani et al., 2002; Morris et al., 1992).

2.2.1 Pitfalls of Manual Evaluation

Grammar judgments decrease when the compression is presented alongside the original sentence. Figure 1 shows that the mean grammar rating for the same compressions is on average about 0.3 points higher when the compression is judged in isolation. Researchers should be careful to state when grammar is judged on compressions lacking reference sentences.

Another factor is the group of judges. Obviously different studies will rely on different judges, so whenever possible the sentences from an existing model should be re-evaluated alongside the new model. The "McD" entries in Table 2 represent a set of sentences generated from the exact same model evaluated by two different sets of judges. The mean grammar and meaning ratings in each evaluation setup differ by 0.5–0.7 points.

3 Compression Rate Predicts Performance

The dominant assumption in compression research is that the system makes the determination about the optimal compression length. For this reason, compression rates can vary drastically across systems. In order to get unbiased evaluations, systems should be compared only when they are compressing at similar rates.

Compression rate is defined as:

$$\frac{\text{\# of tokens in compressed sentence}}{\text{\# of tokens in original sentence}} \times 100 \qquad (1)$$

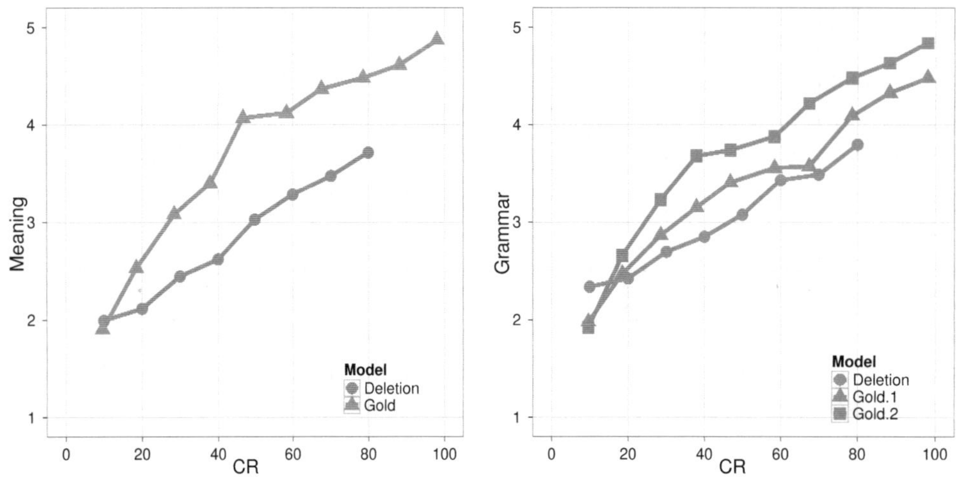

Figure 1: Compression rate strongly correlates with human judgments of meaning and grammaticality. *Gold* represents gold-standard compression and *Deletion* the results of a leading deletion model. Gold.1 grammar judgments were made alongside the original sentence and Gold.2 were made in isolation.

It seems intuitive that sentence quality diminishes in relation to the compression rate. Each word deleted increases the probability that errors are introduced. To verify this notion, we generated compressions at decreasing compression rates of 250 sentences randomly chosen from the written corpus of Clarke and Lapata (2008), generated by our implementation of a leading extractive compression system (Clarke and Lapata, 2008). We collected human judgments using the 5-point scales of meaning and grammar described above. Both quality judgments decreased linearly with the compression rate (see "Deletion" in Figure 1).

As this behavior could have been an artifact of the particular model employed, we next developed a unique gold-standard corpus for 50 sentences selected at random from the same corpus described above. The authors manually compressed each sentence at compression rates ranging from less than 10 to 100. Using the same setup as before, we collected human judgments of these gold standards to determine an upper bound of perceived quality at a wide range of compression rates. Figure 1 demonstrates that meaning and grammar ratings decay more drastically at compression rates below 40 (see "Gold"). Analysis suggests that humans are often able to practice "creative deletion" to tighten a sentence up to a certain point, before hitting a compression barrier, shortening beyond which leads to significant meaning and grammatically loss.

4 Mismatched Comparisons

We have observed that a difference in compression rates as small as 5 percentage points can influence the quality ratings by as much as 0.1 points and conclude: systems must be compared using similar levels of compression. In particular, if system A's output is higher quality, but longer than system B's, then it is not necessarily the case that A is better than B. Conversely, if B has results at least as good as system A, one can claim that B is better, since B's output is shorter.

Here are some examples in the literature of mismatched comparisons:

- Nomoto (2009) concluded their system significantly outperformed that of Cohn and Lapata (2008). However, the compression rate of their system ranged from 45 to 74, while the compression rate of Cohn and Lapata (2008) was 35. This claim is unverifiable without further comparison.
- Clarke and Lapata (2007), when comparing against McDonald (2006), reported significantly better results at a 5-point higher compression rate. At first glance, this does not seem like a remarkable difference. However,

Model	Meaning	Grammar	CompR
C&L	3.83	3.66	64.1
McD	3.94	3.87	64.2
C&L	3.76*	3.53*	78.4*
McD	3.50*	3.17*	68.5*

Table 2: Mean quality ratings of two competing models once the compression rates have been standardized, and as reported in the original work (denoted *). There is no significant improvement, but the numerically better model changes.

> the study evaluated the quality of summaries containing automatically shortened sentences. The average document length in the test set was 20 sentences, and with approximately 24 words per sentence, a typical 65.4% compressed document would have 80 more words than a typical 60.1% McDonald compression. The aggregate loss from 80 words can be considerable, which suggests that this comparison is inconclusive.

We re-evaluated the model described in Clarke and Lapata (2008) (henceforth C&L) against the McDonald (2006) model with global constraints, but fixed the compression rates to be equal. We randomly selected 100 sentences from that same corpus and generated compressions with the same compression rate as the sentences generated by the McDonald model (McD), using our implementation of C&L. Although not statistically significant, this new evaluation reversed the polarity of the results reported by Clarke and Lapata (Table 2). This again stresses the importance of using similar compression rates to draw accurate conclusions about different models.

An example of unbiased evaluation is found in Cohn and Lapata (2009). In this work, their model achieved results significantly better than a competing system (McDonald, 2006). Recognizing that their compression rate was about 15 percentage points higher than the competing system, they fixed the target compression rate to one similar to McDonald's output, and still found significantly better performance using automatic measures. This work is one of the few that controls their output length in order to make an objective comparison (another example is found in McDonald (2006)), and this type of analysis should be emulated in the future.

5 Suggestions

Models should be tested on the same corpus, because different corpora will likely have different features that make them easier or harder to compress. In order to make non-vacuous comparisons of different models, a system also needs to be constrained to produce the same length output as another system, or report results *at least as good* for shorter compressions. Using the multi-reference gold-standard collection described in Section 3, relative performance could be estimated through comparison to the gold-standard curve. The reference set we have annotated is yet small, but this is an area for future work based on feedback from the community.[2]

Other methods for limiting quality disparities introduced by the compression rate include fixing the target length to that of the gold standard (e.g., Unno et al. (2006)). Alternately, results for a system at varying compression levels can be reported,[3] allowing for comparisons at similar lengths. This is a practice to be emulated, if possible, because systems that cannot control output length can make comparisons against the appropriate compression rate.

In conclusion, we have provided justification for the following practices in evaluating compressions:

- Compare systems at similar compression rates.
- Provide results across multiple compression rates when possible.
- Report that system A surpasses B iff: A and B have the same compression rate and A does better than B, or A produces shorter output than B and A does at least as well B.
- New corpora for compression should have multiple gold standards for each sentence.

Acknowledgments

We are very grateful to James Clarke for helping us obtain the results of existing systems and to the reviewers for their helpful comments and recommendations. The first author was supported by the JHU Human Language Technology Center of Excellence. This research was funded in part by the NSF under grant IIS-0713448. The views and findings are the authors' alone.

[2] This data is available on request.

[3] For example, Nomoto (2008) reported results ranging over compression rates: 0.50–0.70.

References

Srinivas Bangalore, Owen Rambow, and Steve Whittaker. 2000. Evaluation metrics for generation. In *Proceedings of the first international conference on Natural language generation-Volume 14*, pages 1–8. Association for Computational Linguistics.

A. Belz and A. Kilgarriff. 2006. Shared-task evaluations in HLT: Lessons for NLG. In *Proceedings of the Fourth International Natural Language Generation Conference*, pages 133–135. Association for Computational Linguistics.

Ted Briscoe. 2006. An introduction to tag sequence grammars and the RASP system parser. *Computer Laboratory Technical Report*, 662.

Chris Callison-Burch, Miles Osborne, and Philipp Koehn. 2006. Re-evaluating the role of Bleu in machine translation research. In *Proceedings of EACL*, Trento, Italy.

James Clarke and Mirella Lapata. 2006. Models for sentence compression: A comparison across domains, training requirements and evaluation measures. In *Proceedings of the 21st International Conference on Computational Linguistics and the 44th annual meeting of the Association for Computational Linguistics*, pages 377–384. Association for Computational Linguistics.

James Clarke and Mirella Lapata. 2007. Modelling compression with discourse constraints. In *Proceedings of the 2007 Joint Conference on Empirical Methods in Natural Language Processing and Computational Natural Language Learning (EMNLP-CoNLL)*, pages 1–11.

James Clarke and Mirella Lapata. 2008. Global inference for sentence compression: An integer linear programming approach. *Journal of Artificial Intelligence Research*, 31:399–429.

Trevor Cohn and Mirella Lapata. 2008. Sentence compression beyond word deletion. In *Proceedings of COLING*.

Trevor Cohn and Mirella Lapata. 2009. Sentence compression as tree transduction. *Journal of Artificial Intelligence Research*, 34:637–674.

Hal Daumé III and Daniel Marcu. 2002. A noisy-channel model for document compression. In *Proceedings of the 40th Annual Meeting on Association for Computational Linguistics*, pages 449–456. Association for Computational Linguistics.

Marie-Catherine de Marneffe and Christopher D. Manning. 2008. Stanford typed dependencies manual.

Bonnie Dorr, David Zajic, and Richard Schwartz. 2003. Hedge trimmer: A parse-and-trim approach to headline generation. In *Proceedings of the HLT-NAACL Workshop on Text summarization Workshop*.

Dimitrios Galanis and Ion Androutsopoulos. 2010. An extractive supervised two-stage method for sentence compression. In *Proceedings of NAACL*.

Michel Galley and Kathleen R. McKeown. 2007. Lexicalized Markov grammars for sentence compression. *the Proceedings of NAACL/HLT*.

Shudong Huang, David Graff, and George Doddington. 2002. Multiple-Translation Chinese Corpus. Linguistic Data Consortium.

Hongyan Jing. 2000. Sentence reduction for automatic text summarization. In *Proceedings of the sixth conference on Applied natural language processing*, pages 310–315. Association for Computational Linguistics.

Kevin Knight and Daniel Marcu. 2000. Statistics-based summarization – Step one: Sentence compression. In *Proceedings of AAAI*.

Kevin Knight and Daniel Marcu. 2002. Summarization beyond sentence extraction: A probabilistic approach to sentence compression. *Artificial Intelligence*, 139:91–107.

LDC. 2005. Linguistic data annotation specification: Assessment of fluency and adequacy in translations. Revision 1.5.

Chin-Yew Lin. 2003. Improving summarization performance by sentence compression: a pilot study. In *Proceedings of the sixth international workshop on Information retrieval with Asian languages-Volume 11*, pages 1–8. Association for Computational Linguistics.

Inderjeet Mani, Gary Klein, David House, Lynette Hirschman, Therese Firmin, and Beth Sundheim. 2002. SUMMAC: a text summarization evaluation. *Natural Language Engineering*, 8(01):43–68.

Erwin Marsi and Emiel Krahmer. 2005. Explorations in sentence fusion. In *Proceedings of the European Workshop on Natural Language Generation*, pages 8–10.

André F. T. Martins and Noah A. Smith. 2009. Summarization with a joint model for sentence extraction and compression. In *Proceedings of the Workshop on Integer Linear Programming for Natural Langauge Processing*.

Ryan McDonald. 2006. Discriminative sentence compression with soft syntactic constraints. In *In Proceedings of EACL*.

Andrew H. Morris, George M. Kasper, and Dennis A. Adams. 1992. The effects and limitations of automated text condensing on reading comprehension performance. *INFORMATION SYSTEMS RESEARCH*, 3(1):17–35.

Courtney Napoles, Chris Callison-Burch, Juri Ganitkevitch, and Benjamin Van Durme. 2011. Paraphrastic sentence compression with a character-based metric: Tightening without deletion. In *Proceedings of ACL, Workshop on Monolingual Text-To-Text Generation*.

Tadashi Nomoto. 2008. A generic sentence trimmer with CRFs. *Proceedings of ACL-08: HLT*, pages 299–307.

Tadashi Nomoto. 2009. A comparison of model free versus model intensive approaches to sentence compression. In *Proceedings of EMNLP*.

E. Reiter and A. Belz. 2006. GENEVAL: A proposal for shared-task evaluation in NLG. In *Proceedings of the Fourth International Natural Language Generation Conference*, pages 136–138. Association for Computational Linguistics.

Stefan Riezler, Tracy H. King, Richard Crouch, and Annie Zaenen. 2003. Statistical sentence condensation using ambiguity packing and stochastic disambiguation methods for lexical-functional grammar. In *Proceedings of the 2003 Conference of the North American Chapter of the Association for Computational Linguistics on Human Language Technology-Volume 1*, pages 118–125. Association for Computational Linguistics.

Yuya Unno, Takashi Ninomiya, Yusuke Miyao, and Jun'ichi Tsujii. 2006. Trimming CFG parse trees for sentence compression using machine learning approaches. In *Proceedings of the COLING/ACL on Main conference poster sessions*, pages 850–857. Association for Computational Linguistics.

Kristian Woodsend, Yansong Feng, and Mirella Lapata. 2010. Generation with quasi-synchronous grammar. In *Proceedings of EMNLP*.

Author Index